Getting the Best from Your
CAMCORDER

Getting the Best from Your
CAMCORDER

Norman Tozer

Regency House ⚮ Publishing Ltd.

Published in 1995 by Regency House
Publishing Limited
The Grange
Grange Yard
London
SE1 3AG

ISBN 1 85361 414 9

Printed & bound by ORIENTAL PRESS, (DUBAI).

Contents

Section 1   Introduction

When home tape recording first came into being cameras and recorders were separate machines. Now they are combined and called **camcorders**. This book is for new and would-be camcorder owners who want to make videos of their family and activities which they would be pleased to show to others. It is also for those who want to improve their video-making skills.

Although camcorders are easy to use, with all the essential controls automated, it does not make them the moving equivalent of the snapshot camera. True, you need not have knowledge of optics or electronics to get the best from them, nor should you get a poorly exposed or unfocused shot. However, because you have the possibility of viewable pictures from the start, it is programme-making skills which require attention and understanding from the beginning.

Video-making is about movement and sound in combination. Its pleasure lies in seeing one and hearing the other, in appreciating how good sound clarifies pictures and how movements can apparently enable you to hear better. Discovering a technique for using video gives you more than a medium of record (although it is a powerful tool in that respect, too); it lets you capture the personalities of friends and family, uniquely revealed in voice and body language as well as the sights and sounds of shared experience.

The book can work for you in various ways. Start at the beginning and find out what the equipment can do for you and how you handle it. Then discover how to use the language of TV and video. Finally, find the ways to start making your own sort of videos. Or dip into the first thing that intrigues you and then turn back to the ways you can achieve it. So – camera running? Action!

Section 2 **Getting to Know your Equipment**

Whether the equipment you choose is expensive or in the budget bracket, it all shares some common principles. This section takes you through the basics of your machine and you will find that you do not need need a degree in electronics to make use of the opportunities it offers. We then discuss whether you should hire, acquire or improvise any other equipment in order to record the range of family activities covered in the book.

VIDEO BASICS

The video camera turns both light and sound into electrical currents. These are then converted to magnetic fields and recorded on the coating of the video tape. To see the recorded pictures the camera reverses the process, creating the currents which become television screen pictures. There are three separate recordings on each video tape: vision, sound and a control track (for maintaining speed and important in editing).

Although video camcorders may seem superficially similar to film or cine cameras they have various features that make them attractively different. First of all, the results they give are instant. Look in the viewfinder, record, then check what you have shot with the instant playback. The tape does not have to be processed and if what you have just done is unsatisfactory you can rewind and record again over the same piece of tape, erasing the previous fault. A mistake or an experiment – you have the result instantly and very economically.

As it is an electronic system, low lighting levels are not a big problem for camcorders. All you do is push a button to increase sensitivity; this boosts the gain in the vision circuit and you can see the effect in the viewfinder before you shoot. The same is true if you wish to change the colouring of a scene (with filters or electronically) or detect lens flare more accurately.

Another difference is in editing – that is, the selection of the material you wish to show, cutting out mistakes or assembling the pictures in a different, more coherent order. Video editing means re-recording only the required sections of sound and picture. Not a

RIGHT
VHS camcorder.

BELOW
Camcorders can be used in low light levels; sensitivity is increased at the press of a button.

BELOW LEFT
VHS-C camcorder.

BELOW RIGHT
8mm camcorder.

difficult procedure but, because the copying and switching of electronic signals reduces their stability, good results need sophisticated equipment. [*See* section The Final Polish.]

THE CAMCORDER – FORMATS

Camcorder controls are very similar to home VCRs, with the familiar Record, Play, Fast Forward, Rewind and Search buttons. Depending on the design and price they can additionally offer many more facilities. So in choosing a camcorder it is important to decide how you intend to use it, or you may find you

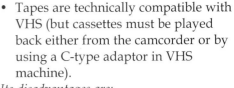

have lots of features you never need but not the one you really want. Your first decision, however, must be – which recording format?

In the domestic equipment market there are currently three main recording formats available in two quality levels – Low and High Band.

LO-BAND QUALITY FORMATS

VHS is the most common home recorder format.
Its advantages are:
- Compatible with other home equipment.
- Easy to swap tapes.
- Tapes can give up to five hours recording time (standard speed).
- Economic tape cost.

Its disadvantages are:
- Tapes and camcorders are bulky.
- Few camcorder models have hi-fi stereo audio systems.
- Some will use tapes over a two-hour length.

VHS-C is the same as VHS but in a smaller, more compact cassette.
Its advantages are:
- More compact camcorders – about a third the weight and size of full size VHS.

- Tapes are technically compatible with VHS (but cassettes must be played back either from the camcorder or by using a C-type adaptor in VHS machine).

Its disadvantages are:
- Not so easy to swap tapes.

8mm is currently the most popular of the three main formats. The cameras use a recording tape 8mm wide in a cassette that looks like, but is actually slightly smaller than, an audio cassette.
Its advantages are:
- Camcorders are small and compact.
- Can record up to two hours on one tape (or up to four hours using LP mode with minimal loss of quality).
- Reasonable tape cost.
- Better quality mono sound than VHS plus Hi-Fi stereo.

Its disadvantage are:
- Not compatible with the VHS.
- Not so easy to swap tapes.
- To play 8mm tapes you connect the camcorder to the aerial or AV socket of your TV (or your VHS machine for copying).

HI-BAND QUALITY FORMATS

Hi8, Super VHS (S-VHS) and S-VHS-C camcorders use special (and more expensive) tapes, producing the best quality recordings. This could be significant for those who intend to edit or copy their tapes as these processes always means a loss of quality; since hi-band tapes start with better quality, copying losses are minimized. To gain the benefit on playback both the mains VCR and the TV must also be hi-band compatible. Although lo-band tapes can be replayed on these machines none of the hi-band tapes will replay on their lo-band counterparts.

A diminishing disadvantage of these hi-band formats is their price.

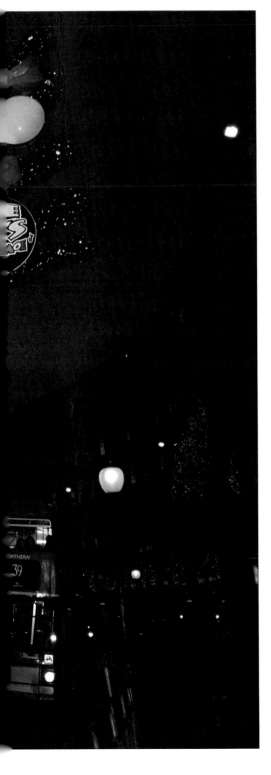

THE CAMCORDER – ESSENTIAL PARTS AND OPTIONAL FACILITIES
The Lens

This focuses light from the scene you are recording onto a CCD (Charge Coupled Device) image sensor (the equivalent of film in a photographic camera). The picture is then turned into electrical impulses.

The lens normally fitted to a camcorder is a zoom – that is technically, a lens with variable focal lengths, meaning you can change the width of the view that it sees. This allows both wide angle and close shots of a subject without either moving the camera or changing lenses.

Beware – camcorder descriptions state the focal range in mm. These figures can only be compared if the different camcorders have the same CCD size.

The range of a zoom is given as a figure multiplied – eg, 10x. This would mean that the closest picture the lens will give would be 10 times closer than the widest view. Very powerful zooms are available (16x and above) which work by enlarging their picture electronically (with a resulting deterioration in quality).

Zoom changes are controlled by pushing a button or rocker switch. Do not be tempted to make these changes in vision – that is, whilst recording. There is rarely a need for such a shot change [*see* next section]. If there is, the zoom movement should be at the speed of and sympathetic to, the subject's movement; however, most zooms start and stop with a jerk and are incapable of variable speeds. The proper use of the zoom switch is to change the length of shot OUT of vision.

FOCUSING – AF (AUTOFOCUS) OR MANUAL

There are several systems for achieving AF. Most focus on objects in the central area of the picture, but all are at their best used out of doors with good daylight and the zoom at its widest.

The Infra-red AF system uses a reflected infra-red beam to measure distance; its accuracy reduces with distant subjects of low reflecting ability. TTL (through the lens) systems are more efficient but are less accurate in poor light or with dark or less contrasty subjects.

Auto-tracking focus is a camcorder

ABOVE
Hi-8 camcorder with the large LCD viewfinder.

BELOW
A zoom lens allows you to get close to people and action.

feature which keeps the AF mechanism locked onto a subject whilst it moves around the frame.

EXPOSURE

Too much light through the lens means the pictures will be overexposed – that is bright or bleached out. If too little light is let through the lens, the resulting underexposure gives gloomy shots with details lost. The main method of exposure control on a camcorder is the aperture or iris, which opens and closes just like the iris of the eye.

Camcorder exposure control is usually automatic. Most machines have *backlight compensation* which lets in more light to cope with shooting against the light. Other machines now have *programmed exposure* which offers you presets to deal with specific conditions (eg, 'sunlight' or 'sports').

SENSITIVITY TO LIGHT

Camcorder manufacturers often quote a 'minimum lux' – that is, a measure of the lowest light level in which they can operate. Currently minimum figures are given of between one and 10, often obtained by boosting the gain of the vision circuit. The light level in sunlight can be 30,000 lux – a 150 watt bulb in your living room at night could be around 300 lux and engineers say that 1000-2000 lux is the minimum needed for watchable pictures. Whatever the actual figures, pictures recorded by these extremely low illumination levels are noisy (grainy) and lack colour, making them very difficult to copy and edit.

FAST SHUTTER SPEEDS

Camcorders record their pictures at the equivalent of 25 pictures per second, giving an exposure of 1/25 of a second. Many manufacturers offer a feature of extremely high 'shutter speeds' – between 1/1000 and 1/10,000 of a second. This phenomenon is used for recording fast action pictures with the intention that they will be sharp in still-frame or slow motion.

As in still photography, a picture taken at 1/25 of a second of a fast-moving object produces a blurred image. If you playback a video picture of a fast moving subject at normal speed there is no problem – the illusion of movement is satisfactory. But if you use the Pause control to look at single images they will be blurred. Only if you record at 1/1000

of a second or more will the images be 'frozen' without blurring.

However, the considerable reduction in the time that light can pass through the lens may produce unwanted 'side effects' such as:

- These sharper images may replay in a jerky, stroboscopic way at normal speed.
- The pictures may be underexposed. As the amount of light admitted has been greatly reduced by the shorter exposure time, the aperture (iris) opens to admit more light to compensate. The problem comes if the light available is not strong enough for adequate exposure.
- The pictures will have a very shallow focus because of the much wider aperture. Especially with autofocus, this can result in a fast moving subject being poorly focused.

WHITE BALANCE.

Look at this page of the book in sunlight. Carry it to the shade and look at it again; then look at it under artificial light. What colour is the paper? If you thought it was white under all those different conditions your brain was doing a marvellous, although everyday act, of colour compensation. Video cameras can do the same but with less sophistication. The paper may be white but will only appear so under white light, usually sunlight. In the shade the paper would turn a pale blue, reflecting the sky. And in artificial light, it turns yellow, reflecting the colour of the burning tungsten filament (or a shade of green if the light is fluorescent).

The camcorder's *white balance* controls are meant to reproduce colours

the way our eyes see them no matter what the colour of the light falling on them. Usually they are automatic (AWB) and continuously make white appear as white under all lighting conditions. Since they can overcompensate in some circumstances, there are usually two additional controls preset to balance white under daylight (or outdoor) and artificial light (or indoor). The daylight control should be used when you want varying light conditions to be visible (eg, the pleasing glow on faces of evening light). The artificial light preset could be used when there was mixed light (eg, faces lit by lamps but some daylight seen in a window).

White balance systems assess light using one of two different methods. The first is a sensor on the camera body which measures the colour of the light falling on the camera (it works well

TOP
Sports fans can use fast shutter speeds to get sharp slow motion and still frames to analyze their performance.

ABOVE
The faces of this couple have a blue cast because they are under shady trees. Using the white balance would correct this.

unless the light falling on the camera is different from the light on the scene). The second is a sensor which works through the lens (fine again, but inclined to be overinfluenced if there are large areas of a single colour within the picture, producing an erroneous compensating colour cast).

A manual override overcomes these difficulties. [*See* section Using Your Equipment.]

VIEWFINDERS

The viewfinder is an important and basic part of the camcorder and some thought should be given to it before buying any particular model. It is not optical (like a still camera) but electronic, displaying what is being seen through the taking lens on a miniature monitor screen. It is therefore important that it should be accurate and comfortable to use, or you will never be able to compose your shots properly. It may project from the machine or be built into the body; whichever, check if it is comfortable for you and that you can adjust it for your own eyesight. Since you spend much of your time with your eye to it, the viewfinder is also used to give a great deal of information concerning the state of the camcorder. Its symbols and word displays will tell you of its readiness for use or warn you of the state of the batteries.

Viewfinders can be both small and large and display in black and white or colour. Some LCD (Liquid Crystal Display) colour viewfinders are not very sharp and are therefore difficult to use to judge picture focus; large ones are difficult to use in bright light.

RECORDING SPEEDS

Most camcorders allow double the running time of tape by offering an alternative slower recording speed. Recordings made in Long Play mode are always visually inferior to those in Standard Play.

Timelapse and *Animation* are two features which mean that the camera can change from its continuous running to record single frames of information at pre-arranged intervals. This is the way that cartoons are made or inanimate objects appear to move. Alternatively use it to make the sun rise in 30 seconds or see a tent put up in one minute.

FADERS

These allow pictures to be faded in or out from black (or white) and sound from and to silence. This in-camera system means that you do not have to use additional equipment to create this effect [*See* TV language in section Telling a Story].

CHARACTER GENERATORS

These let you create your own titles in the camera. Superimposers let you copy prepared titles.

IMAGE STABILIZERS

These are built-in systems which help to keep the recorded picture steady if the camera is subjected to bumps or vibration [*see* Steadicam on page 15].

A BUILT-IN LIGHT

This is available on some camcorders; it can overcome some of the problems of shooting at low light levels but can produce others, such as destroying the atmosphere of any existing lighting or overlighting objects closer to the camera than the subject. Built-in lights use up battery power faster.

DATA DISPLAY

This is the ability to record in vision a date and time (and sometimes a few words); it is featured on most camcorders.

Viewfinders are important; many are flexible allowing you to see in awkward positions and most have some sight correction.

Animation and timelapse facilities let you make your own cartoons.

SOUND

Sound quality should never be overlooked – always try to monitor it whilst recording.

Camcorders record in either mono or stereo. For most family videos mono sound is adequate since it will be replayed on television sets which reproduce in mono. If you think you will want to edit, consider camcorders which offer stereo or hi-fi tracks in addition to the normal (linear) mono track.

Camcorders have attached or built-in microphones. These are of variable quality and tend to pick up as much sound from the camcorder and your handling of it as from the scene you are recording. For any improvement to your soundtrack you will need an external microphone and therefore a microphone socket for plugging it in (regrettably absent from many models).

The control of sound recording volume on a camcorder is normally automatic. Although this is one less thing to worry about during recording it has drawbacks, such as:

- The system increases the level of all sounds it has difficulty in hearing, so if no one speaks for a moment it increases the background buzz.
- Sudden loud sounds cause the automatic system to turn down the volume, sometimes for a few seconds, rendering any following voices briefly inaudible.

Audio dub is a facility essential for any editing or sound refinement process as it lets you re-record the soundtrack without interfering with the picture.

Battery dischargers help overcome the problem of partly full batteries. This facility may be available on some chargers or can be bought separately.

Ensure that there is an earphone socket on the camcorder – this is essential for monitoring during recording.

EDITING

If you wish to copy or edit your recordings look for camcorders which have suitable facilities – then ensure that you understand them! They must give separate control of the audio and video channels and for more sophisticated editing you will need facilities which let you connect the camcorder to, and control it from, other equipment. Look for the following facilities:

- *Insert edit* lets you record new picture material over existing material with minimal frame-roll or picture disturbance.
- *Edit search* is a frame-by-frame search system which assists accurate editing.

It is also the term for a playback search possible within Record Standby mode.

- *A Built-in edit controller* controls insert edits by the use of a counter.
- *Index Search, Scan and Marking* is a system that lets you electronically mark specific tape sections, allowing easy access to these parts of your recording. Used for editing; it is a more widely available alternative to *Timecode* (see below).
- *Timecode* is a reference number given to each frame as it is recorded. It can be made visible on the picture or on a separate counter to log and find specific shots for editing.
- *Edit control terminals* allow you to plug in a variety of edit controllers [*see* section The Final Polish].
- *Remote control* is available for most of these facilities.

ANCILLARY EQUIPMENT
Batteries
Although camcorders can operate from mains electricity most people use batteries. To date they have usually been the nickel-cadmium type and they are regarded with dissatisfaction by some users. They work best when used regularly, run until they are completely flat and recharged slowly. In practice this rarely happens. For instance, camcorders never completely discharge a battery; to let you get your tape out of the machine, the safety cut-out may operate when there is still a quarter of the charge left in the battery. If you then recharge (or top-up recharge) it produces a 'memory effect'. This means that if you do not use all the charge the battery thinks you will never want it, and as a result increasingly under charges it, until it eventually refuses to take any charge.

Battery dischargers help overcome the problem of partly full batteries. They may be made as part of a charger or purchased separately.

Battery belts and shoulder packs are several batteries linked, giving more stable current and for longer power times; some provide power from several outputs. They give you and the camera freedom of movement.

Microphones
There are two basic types:
*   Dynamic – needs no power to operate it and is easy to shield from wind noise.
*   Electret – uses batteries and is more sensitive to some sounds. Useful for indoors.

You have to decide which pick-up pattern you require. Microphones (mics) are made to hear from particular directions. Omni-directional ones hear sounds equally well from all around them; uni-directional ones (sometimes called cardioid) favour sounds from specific directions while those intended to pick up more distant sounds from their fronts only are referred to as Rifles. Use omni-directional mics when background or ambient sound levels are low or where they can be placed very close to the sound source and use directional mics to select sounds from higher ambient levels, vocal solos or street interviews.

Microphones can also be made to hear only parts of the sound spectrum – high pitched sounds, low frequency ones

Mixing several soundtracks through a mixer adds sophistication, even when you edit pictures in-camera.

A lapel (or personal) mic – the switch box can be put in a pocket out of sight.

or just in the mid-range. These have specialist uses; eg, if a low frequency range mic is used for a drum it will pick up less of other instruments alongside it which would be making higher pitched sounds. Other mics can be made to hear high and mid range sounds – good for recording people speaking in a noisy street; the low frequency traffic sounds will not be recorded and you will hear the voices more clearly.

Microphones can be large and sensitive to handling; some are intended to be hand-held, others (personals) are small enough to be pinned on clothing while larger ones need to be supported on stands. Although the best results are obtained from mics connected by cables, radio mics are appearing at lower prices and giving greater reliability.

Earphones are necessary for you to check sound during recording and playback on location. Use the large 'closed back' type, to ensure that other sounds are blocked out and the sound you hear has come from the microphone only. Earplug-types and the lightweight earphones from personal stereos are unsatisfactory and can cause 'feedback howl'.

When choosing mics and headphones make sure that they match the circuitry of your camcorder (or other equipment you intend to hook up together) by matching its wiring type –

Typical closed-back earphones.

balanced or unbalanced – or its impedance. The camcorder dealer should assist you with this.

Sound Mixers
Sound mixers allow you to record from several sources at the same time; voices can be recorded at the same time as music, and sound effects can be added to your original sound recorded on location. If you have a mic input on your camcorder, a suitable mixer could be used to blend the sounds from several mics to make the original recording. Or you could use one afterwards to replace your original camcorder sounds.

Sometimes mixers are made with input channels which accept microphones only (useful for recording onto the camcorder); more often they will have one or two channels which will accept the sound from mics and others which are for pre-recorded sources – audio cassette players, CD players or other VCRs. Most useful are those which have switchable channels, accepting either mics or pre-recorded sources. Another feature of more expensive mixers is a visual recording meter to show you the level of sounds you are recording. This is useful as it enables you to preset the channel controls, making the balancing of different sounds much easier.

Beware – if you buy or hire a sound mixer ensure that its output matches the recorder you want to use it with. Next check that its input channels will accept the type of microphone or player you want to record from. Last, that it will operate from mains and battery.

OTHER ACCESSORY EQUIPMENT
Tripods
These are a necessity to keep your pictures steady. Bumpy, unsteady shots distract from the subject matter. When cameras were large and bulky, heavy tripods were necessary because muscle fatigue caused unsteadiness; now that camcorders are light tripods are still necessary to prevent wobbly shots – it is difficult to maintain steadiness with light machines, especially in high winds or amongst crowds.

A tripod comprises two main parts:
- The three-legged stand, in which the legs should be strong and steady or braced to give rigidity. A geared centre column helps give a quick height adjustment without having to reset the legs.
- The head which must be firmly fixed to the tripod and which supports the camera enabling pan and tilt movements. A fluid head is best, allowing the smoothest moves – some drag helps prevent jerking. The most useful type of head has a quick release plate which releases the camcorder quickly for hand-held shots. To give rigid support the camcorder is screwed to the tripod head base plate but the quick release avoids screwing and unscrewing, enabling the base plate (with camera) to be released from the tripod by moving only one or two catches. Heads with a spirit level are invaluable for framing a level picture, whatever the surface.

A *Dolly* is a wheeled frame for supporting a camera to take moving shots over smooth ground. *Rolling wheels* fix to a tripod for the same purpose.

The *Steadicam JR* is a semi-professional version of a device for keeping cameras steady when travelling over irregular surfaces for hand-held moving shots. Although expensive, like most video equipment, it can be hired.

Other supports include the *monopod* (light and easy to transport and a useful tripod substitute) and *shoulder* and *chest braces*.

With any camera supporting device, check if it will:
- Let you see the camcorder's viewfinder.
- Let you take shots at any lens height.
- Take the weight of your equipment.

LIGHTS
There is great choice of video lights; some are powered directly from the camcorder, some have their own battery system and others are intended to be used off-camera and mains powered. Many are intended to be mounted on the camera accessory shoe

SUPPLEMENTARY LENSES AND LENS ATTACHMENTS
You may want these for achieving wider or closer shots.

FILTERS
These are required for changing picture colours, reducing haze or reflections, or simply turning highlights into patterns.

HIRING

Until you have owned a camcorder for some time and discover how you like to use it, resist buying accessories for occasional use; most can be hired when you need them. This will provide experience of using different accessories without committing you to them permanently.

Enquire at a specialist (who may offer both domestic and professional equipment), a television rental company or your local video dealer.

Ask about:

• Camera mountings for special occasions – tripods (plus special high or low ones), dollies, monopods, quality fluid heads with levelling, steadicams.
• Lights, stands, or lighting kits.
• All types of sound equipment – sound mixers, mics, mic stands and booms, quality headphones, equalizers, extra cables.
• Editing and post-production equipment [*see* section The Final Polish].

When making your enquiry check:

• The rates per day, per week, weekend, or other period.
• Does the price include tax (like VAT)?
• What amount and in what form do they require a deposit?
• What is the time period – does a 'day' mean any 24 hours or only from a specific morning hour?
• That the hirer knows what equipment you intend to use with his, to ensure that it will match and function correctly.

Also, try to look over some of his stock items, to form an impression of how well they are kept and serviced – are they piled up in a backroom, or individually bagged, or kept in custom made cases?

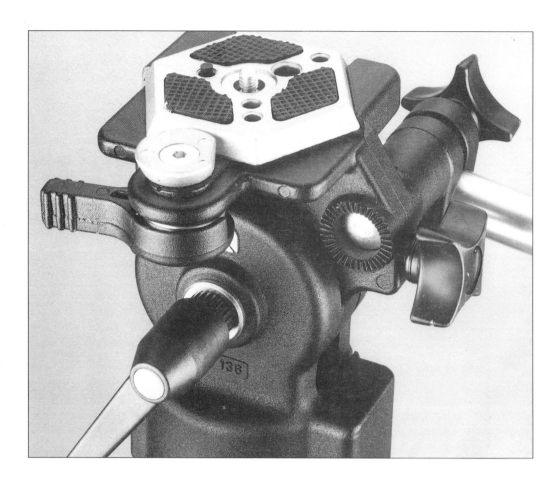

TOP
Tripod head with a typical quick release plate for video cameras.

RIGHT
Tripods with a geared centre column. This allows a quick height adjustment without the need to reset the legs.

Section 3 The Ingredients – Light Exposure, Focus and Composition

LIGHT

Our eyes are drawn towards light. Unconsciously, we use brightness and darkness, the direction of shadow and the colour of light to give us information about distance, shape and time. For good pictures, however, you need to be able to observe and appreciate light consciously.

Light has intensity, direction and colour. Intensity is easy to understand when we see sunlight – the source is visible, its deep shadows obscure. But the atmosphere refracts light, scattering it as it passes through, and so many surfaces reflect light that there is hardly a time when a shadow is obscure, when we cannot see some detail in it. However, the technology of photography makes us choose what to do; there are occasions when it will not allow us to show what is happening both in the light and the shadow. Is the true picture the bright one, when we can see virtually nothing in the shadow, or do we want to show the details in the shade with all the highlights 'burned out' and featureless? Can there be a compromise?

The direction from which light falls suggests a time of day but it also gives things shape, revealing or distorting objects. Varying lights playing on a face can ask us to believe different things about a person's character. If the light is very high, cheekbones become prominent and the jaw looks firmer but it causes dark eye sockets, emphasizes bags under the eyes and any wrinkles. What sort of person is that?

ABOVE and BELOW LEFT
Light has intensity, direction and colour.

BELOW
Light can reveal or obscure; is the true image the tree branches, or the background houses?

17

As the light source is lowered, so the wrinkles are less obvious but the face becomes flatter and fuller, the jawline softer and the eyes more apparent. Has the personality changed? Or, with the light falling from one side, only one eye is visible, one ear dominates that side of the head and the nose, catching the light, seems large. Is the light now being deceiving or revealing?

The colour of light is even more difficult to see objectively, our brains tend to normalize it. We may enjoy seeing people in the evening sunset but do we also notice the blue cast over faces in the shade on a bright day, or the green cast caused by fluorescent lights? And do we ever notice how yellow our faces have become as we step into the light of our domestic lamps?

Light can be controlled. Most obviously, artificial lights can be used of more or less power and moved to different positions. But much can also be done in daylight; it can be shaded, it can be filtered through cloth, it can be reflected, and its power can be increased or decreased by the distance and type of reflecting surface – even its height and direction can be changed. Alternatively,

Character revealed by light – (1) strong or harsh?

if you do not change the light source you could move the subject; turning it away from or towards the light could change its apparent shape. Or changes could be made by moving the camera, perhaps altering the relationship of light between the foreground and the background.

If you can learn to 'see' light and its effects you can begin to control the pictures you record.

(2) soft and gentle?

A Checklist for light
- Is there enough light to produce the sort of picture you want?
- Is it hard or soft?
- Does it define the subject making it the correct shape?
- Can you see enough detail?
- Does the colour of the light look right?
- Will the picture improve if you change the light? If so, should the subject move, or the camera, or the light?

WHITE BALANCE

Setting a white balance should be done each time you change a location or light conditions. It is all too easy to find that a daylight sequence has recorded with a blue cast because you left the setting on indoor or that a whole indoor sequence has become yellow because you left the setting on outdoor.

Some camcorders only let you to switch from indoor to outdoor settings but if there is a manual setting follow the procedure outlined below. Take a piece of white paper or card and hold it in the scene, catching the light that will fall on the setting and the people in it. Zoom in to fill the viewfinder with the card (there is no need to focus it), then press the white balance button until the viewfinder sign 'white' (or your camcorder's equivalent) stops flashing. Colour should now be rendered naturally.

The advantage of setting a white balance manually is that you can choose how to colour a scene. If you prefer a cold look to the scenes you want to shoot, instead of a white card for the setting procedure, try using a pale yellow, pink or red one. These colours will cause the camera to tint the shots various shades of blue. You will need to do your own trials to find the most suitable for your purpose. Equally, if you want a warmer feeling to scenes, white balance using blue shades thereby tricking the camera into tinting the pictures pink or yellow.

The colours of light – (1) Blue shade in daylight; see the difference from the patch of sunlight at the top. (Monastery, Mount Athos, Greece.)

ABOVE
(3) Green, fluorescent lighting. (Metro station, Washington D.C.)

RIGHT
(2) Yellow, artificial light. (Young Vic Theatre performance.)

EXPOSURE

Camcorders usually control the exposure automatically (AE), opening or closing the iris – or lens aperture – to let in more or less light. Although this system is meant to prevent over or underexposed pictures there can be unwanted side effects.

Automatic exposure can only make an average exposure of the scene – this may not be what you want since it allows no choice between showing detail in the bright or dark areas.

As the camera moves (or people and things move within the picture) the dark and light areas change within it, altering the exposure. This causes movement of the iris which has an unsettling effect on the viewer. For example, a group of people are standing in bright shade; the picture would have a reasonable balance of detail and the faces would be seen, but if the original group are joined by others wearing white or pale colours the auto-exposure system would close the iris, darkening the faces and blackening the shadows.

BACKLIGHT CONTROL

This should be used in situations where the area behind the head is lighter than the face, to prevent the face being seen in silhouette. It can also be used where you need to see more detail in shadows.

ABOVE
(N) The system cannot decide whether to expose for the face or the window behind. Use backlight control to expose for the face.

LEFT
Side effects of AE. The camera cannot reproduce the range of brightness in this scene so the system has overexposed the floor area.

FOCUS

The subject – that is, the object or person you want the viewer to see – should be in focus (sharp) at all times. Remember that if the subject is a person it is the eyes that should always be in focus.

If the subject moves (closer to or further away from the camera) you or the automatic focusing system (AF) should adjust the focus. Bear in mind that autofocus does not always focus where you want it to. It is best to learn how to focus for yourself.

Autofocus systems may be particularly confused when:

- The subject reflects little light because it is dark.
- There is something between you and the subject, such as the bars of a cage when shooting a zoo animal.
- There are bright surfaces in the picture with the subject, such as a glass window between the camera and the subject or water – a stream or river – in the composition itself but not the subject.
- There are rapidly moving vertical objects in the picture, eg, people in a crowd. This situation causes a visually unsettling phenomenon known as 'focus hunting'. As the objects are simultaneously moving closer to and further from the camera the AF system cannot decide where to settle so it continually shifts the plane of focus towards and away from the camera.

To focus a zoom lens: zoom in on the subject as close as your camera will allow, focus the subject sharply (on the eyes if it is a person) and zoom out to the length of shot required. Then, whether you zoom in or out, the subject remains in focus – PROVIDED that the subject does not then move closer to or further from the camera.

ABOVE
Modern camcorders can focus on subjects very close without the need to switch to the Macro, (very close focussing) facility, allowing this couple to record themselves.

RIGHT
Typically difficult AF situation; the system may hunt for focus between the flamingoes and the foreground wire cage.

DEPTH OF FOCUS

The side effects of iris changes

Opening or closing the iris (or aperture) not only affects exposure but the depth of focus as well. When the iris is wide open there is little depth of focus, that is, hardly anything in front or behind the subject you have focused on will be sharp. But when the iris is closed down the depth increases making objects appear sharp for a considerable distance in front of and behind the subject. It follows that on bright days pictures will have much greater depth than on dull ones. As you may not always want this effect there are two techniques to overcome this.

The effect of the zoom

The depth of focus also changes as you zoom in and out. With the zoom at wide it will show greater depth than when at tele (zoomed in). For more depth in a shot, stand close to the subject and zoom out to wide; for less, move away from the subject and zoom in to tele.

Remember :

- With shallow depth of focus, keeping the picture continuously sharp is vital; whenever the subject goes out of focus it will be very noticeable.
- Shots zoomed in to the narrowest angle of the lens are more difficult to keep steady; use a tripod or other camera support.

Neutral density filters

If there is too much light for the scene you want to shoot and you wish to reduce the depth of focus (with the zoom at its widest), use a neutral density filter. This simply reduces the amount of light entering the lens but has no other effect on the nature or colour of light.

COMPOSITION

Most people do not compose a picture consciously; a few can do it instinctively but most of us must learn. It would be unusual for someone to stop at a view or a crowd of people and think what wonderful ovals, circles or triangular shapes they would form in a picture. What mostly happens when we see landscapes or fairgrounds is that we are awed or thrilled by the sight, sound and smell and just aim the camera. Then, when we see the result – dull, distant hills or insignificantly small people standing in front of the big wheel – we are disappointed and frustrated. How did we lose the majesty or the excitement? The answer is probably by faulty composition.

Good composition draws your eyes into the picture, moves them around with an energy which reflects the subject and also lets you pick up more details on the way. It may keep your eyes moving or let them rest somewhere, but how?

In everyday life our eyes constantly explore the surroundings and are always drawn towards the light. The same happens when we look at a screen – automatically we seek the brightest light or colour. Our eyes are helped in this process if they have lines to follow – and a line is only visible because it contrasts with its background. These lines and areas of light and dark are naturally of more interest to us if we recognize them as familiar things – houses, trees, people. But when they are assembled and confined as an image we are also more satisfied if they make certain patterns; our senses seem to prefer triangles and circular shapes.

The best way to learn about composition is to examine photographs or paintings. Find the light areas and connect them. What shapes are made? Where in the frame – central or off-centre – are these light areas or areas of most interest? Or do they obey the rule of thirds – that is, are they placed one- or two-thirds up the frame and one- or two-thirds across the frame?

COMPOSING WITH YOUR CAMCORDER

Move your camera so that the subject is in the centre of the picture, or where the lines of composition in the picture meet, or in the lightest area. Isolate the subject from other objects, or control the focus to make it the only sharp part of the picture.

LEFT
Circular composition.

RIGHT

Move the camera or the subject so that the eyes are two-thirds of the way up the screen. Try to compose shots so that there are no distracting lines, colours or objects in either the foreground or background of your picture. Make sure that objects like lamp-posts, plants or trees are not immediately behind heads or ears or it will look as if they are growing from the person! Move either the camera or the subject to avoid this.

LEFT

If a face is not the lightest area in the frame, try to make sure that dark areas are behind the head and away from the direction it is facing; lighter areas are best in front of it. Move the subject or the camera to achieve this.

RIGHT and FAR LEFT

Lines, like those made by pathways or shadows slanting across the frame, can be used to draw attention to the area of most interest. Converging lines are more interesting than parallel ones – they suggest more energy (they also form triangles). Curving lines have more life in them than straight ones (they also form ovals and circles).

LEFT
Try to compose in depth as well as laterally; an illusion of depth is pleasing in the screen picture. To suggest it, use objects in the foreground (and background) which suggest a sense of scale. Let any lines in the picture run from the camera to the distance, not across the frame.

BELOW LEFT
Especially in closer shots, if someone is shown looking or moving left or right it is best not to place the head in the centre of the frame. Have a space or 'looking room' on the side of the frame the person is looking towards or the picture will seem cramped.

AND FINALLY, PICTURE CLARITY DEPENDS ON:
- Focus and Resolution – the sharpness and amount of light.
- Good composition and design means being able to differentiate easily between the subject and the rest of the picture because: the subject is sharp, its colour stands apart from the other colours, the lines of the composition lead the eye to it and the eye is also led to it because it is brighter (the eye always seeks the lightest part of a picture first).

CAMCORDER OPERATION
HOLDING THE CAMCORDER

Keep the height of your camcorder lens at the same level as your subject's eyes. Only look up or down at someone if you have a reason for creating a dramatic effect.

Most camcorders are light and easy to hold, but two aspects of camera operation need special attention: keeping shots steady and level, and the use of the viewfinder.

Keeping a camera steady takes practice. To keep the picture level use this procedure: look in the viewfinder and find a horizontal line in your composition, then pan up or down to place it so that it runs along the top or bottom of the frame. When you see that the two are parallel carefully recompose, preserving the relationship of the horizontal with the edge of the viewfinder frame. Naturally, no one can keep a picture level and steady all the time – it may be windy or we may be jostled in a crowd; a camera support (one with a spirit level) can cure both such problems.

Using a viewfinder also requires practice; people are puzzled when they replay their tapes to see heads cut off and other signs of poor composition. This is usually caused by not putting the eye properly to the viewfinder cup so that you can see all edges of the frame. Also check that you can see to focus properly; viewfinders usually can adjust to correct for each individual's sight – if your camera does not consult your retailer about a sight correction attachment. Finally, try not to close one eye when using the viewfinder – at least not all the time; you may need to when first setting the shot but after that keep both eyes open. In this way you see what is about to happen and can make smooth adjustments to the framing when necessary.

Some cameras have movable viewfinders making it easier to frame shots from unusual angles.

Camcorders are easy to hold.

Keep shots steady. This enthusiast is supporting his elbow.

MOVEMENTS

Remember:

- All camera movements and shot changes should be unnoticed by the viewer and be patterned on normal head and eye movements.
- When the camera mounting stays still but the camera pivots sideways on the head this is called **a Pan** (left or right).
- When the camera mounting stays still but the camera pivots up and down on its head this is called a **Tilt** (up or down).
- When the camera moves closer to, or further away from, the subject, the movements are described as a **Track** (in or out).
- When the camera moves sideways parallel to its subject it is described as **Crabbing** (left or right).
- The effect of moving closer to, or away from, a subject is obtained by a picture change called a **Zoom** (in or out). In this case the camera does not move; instead the operator moves a part of the lens.

MAKING CAMERA MOVES HOLDING YOUR CAMCORDER

Always plan how you want to end the shot and your movement.

To pan – stand facing the direction you wish to finish the sequence, then twist your body to where the shot starts. This ensures that you end in a stable position.

To tilt – whether your movement is down or up, keep your eye to the viewfinder and lift or pull down with the elbows.

To crane – as if the camera was on a column, practise the move by bending or straightening the knees.

To track or crab – get someone to guide you to prevent falling; be aware that if you walk in an ordinary way the camera will rise and fall with your movement. Whether you need to move forwards, backwards or sideways, walk with bent knees so that they act as a shock absorber. Do these moves with the zoom at its widest – it minimizes irregularity in your movements. (The faster you need to crab or track the more you need special support; it is worth experimenting with improvised or DIY devices.)

Tips to Try

- For cameras without image stabilizers, to keep someone in shot who is moving fast or over irregular ground try walking or running with them with the camera suspended in a sling using a vest or a fabric with some 'give'.
- For tracking shots over smooth ground try holding your camcorder sitting in a wheelchair or well-balanced trolley.

Using the zoom lens

The zoom is a convenient way to change the framing of a shot unseen (out-of-vision); its other use is as a dramatic effect in-vision. Remember that all picture changes must be motivated – the reason for the change must be apparent within the shot.

The zoom alters the picture's character, so use it sparingly. Exposure changes during zooming, altering the depth of focus. Often the resolution (sharpness) changes, and so too will the straightness of horizontal and vertical shapes, especially towards the edge of the picture. These abnormal visual changes have no place in ordinary recording, nor does fast zooming, zooming to alter the

BELOW
Some cameras have movable viewfinders making it easier to frame shots from unusual angles.

angle of view considerably or continuous zooming – all are unnatural head or eye movements. However, all these have a use when your intention is to shock, disorientate or physically sicken the viewer. Use them advisedly!

AN EXAMPLE OF AN ACCEPTABLE ZOOM IN-VISION:

A moment in the programme where your interest is such that you would naturally lean forward, either cut to a closer shot, track or zoom in. If the effect is to be natural, the track or zoom should be a small, imperceptible move.

To zoom in or out from a subject is a small, but special, skill which repays practice. To start from a long shot and finish on a medium close-up cannot be done at the press of a button. If you are framing in the usual way the long shot will be composed with the subject's head two-thirds of the way up the frame; when you finish the subject's eyes should still be two-thirds of the way up the frame. This means that to keep a natural-seeming space at the top of the frame you must tilt up all the time you zoom in. The reverse is also true – tilt down as you zoom out.

Remember :
If you intend to edit, all shots with camera movements (especially pans and zooms) should be shot with a few seconds stationary before and after the move in addition to the run in and run out times. (This allows choice in editing – if the movement is not suitable you can use the static part of the shot.)

Heavier cameras sometimes make steady zooming easier.

Keep the eye height constant in the frame whilst zooming.

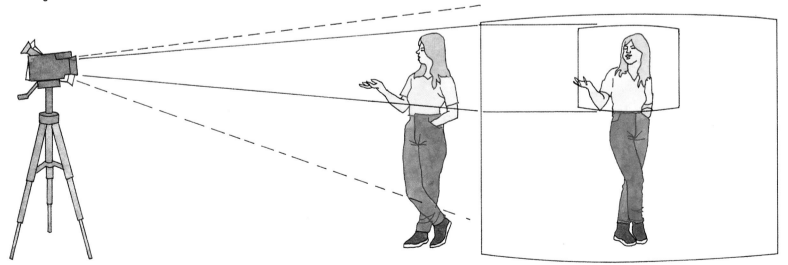

SETTING UP A MONITOR SCREEN

For shooting and editing, to check that your camera or your tapes are reproducing colour well you will need to monitor them on your TV screen. Unless you use an expensive graded monitor your TV will only approximate true colour; but it will be a good guide if you set it up correctly.

You will need a true colour source, preferably electronically generated, like the vertical colour bars which professional equipment can originate. You may find it useful to get these recorded on a separate tape especially for this purpose. A less satisfactory alternative is to make up your own colour test card – a 30 x 22cm black card over which you stick patches of primary colour.

With the colour source being fed to the monitor, the following adjustments should be done in a dimly lit room:

- Turn down to zero the contrast, brightness and colour controls.
- Turn up the brilliance until the black bar can be seen as the last step.
- Turn up the contrast until the steps between bars are even.
- Turn up the colour until all the colours look correct – that is, matching the original (not your own preference for pale or saturated colours).

Using an external plug-in directional mic for an interview. (Note: it is pointed at the mouth.)

SOUND

If you want to achieve the best pictures you need also to record good sound. Bad sound makes the pictures look poor; good sound makes them look great. Just as some voices can be heard more clearly when you see the face, many pictures make more sense when accompanied by clear and relevant sounds.

Whatever preparations you have made for recording sound, do listen both before you shoot to check if you can improve things and while you shoot to make adjustments. For example, during recording there might be a sound channel break-up or wind rumble on a mic. Knowing this means that you can retake (or continue) until you have what you need. The delay of checking after the take means that the action may have passed and be lost.

Use closed back headphones to monitor the sound from your mics and playback. They cut out ambient location sound and ensure that what you hear is what you want.

Use the mic attached to the camera only if you are sure that it does not pick up the sounds of the camcorder or your handling of it. In those circumstances use it to pick up ambient sounds, maybe for later re-recording. Alternatively, it might be possible to use it for speech, but with the speaker close to camera and on a quiet location with little or no background noise.

The best advice is for anything other than background sound use an external mic plugged in to the camcorder, or, if you have several sound sources, several mics plugged into a mixer which in turn is plugged into the camcorder.

If you want someone to speak directly to the camera or to record a conversation between two people your choice of mic is conditioned by the level of noise around your subjects. For one person the lapel mic (or 'personal') is probably the best choice; its small size means that attached to clothing within 35 cms of the mouth it is least noticeable and should give reasonable sound in all but the heaviest of traffic or industrial noise. This type of mic is usually omni-directional and outdoors it should be used with a windshield. To prevent speakers from blowing into it, try attaching it upside down at an angle.

The alternative, and also the choice for most interview situations, is a directional, hand-held mic. With a windshield it can be used outdoors and, if necessary, fairly close to speakers; the interviewer can aim it at each participant and it will cut down on background noise. But avoid the mistake of 'working close' in a location with little background noise; if speakers are too close the background is lost leaving no sense of atmosphere. In many indoor situations such a single mic could be placed on a stand between the participants where it is less obtrusive.

There are two other situations where a special microphone can record the voice clearly despite background noise. The first is at public gatherings, such as processions and sports occasions where you wish to record an out-of-vision commentator simultaneously. Here you will need a mic placed in front of the mouth. Currently, headsets with combined earphone/mic facilities are available and especially useful for people who wish to speak their own commentary whilst operating the camera.

Another situation which needs careful microphone selection is where you have high background noise but the speakers are in vision. Using mics in front of their mouths looks ugly; use instead the ultra-directional mic – the rifle. These accept sounds from a narrow angle for some distance in front of them and substantially reduce the sound accepted from the sides. The best situation is to have someone to help operate them as they should be pointed carefully at the speaker and hopefully kept out of picture. Failing this, try fixing them to a stand or as a last resort to the camera accessory shoe.

The rifle mic's abilty to record clear sounds with minimal background works well in a rather different recording situation – drama. Because you need a high degree of control over all elements of your recording it is not desirable to have voices, or any other featured sounds, recorded with noticeable atmospheres. If these are needed they should be restored in post-production where their dramatic potential can be explored within exact limits.

Seeing the mic in vision – pinned to clothing, obscuring a singer's mouth or isolated on a stand – may not always be what the style of your video requires. There are occasions when you may not wish to see it in vision at all. Hiding it behind a vase of flowers is fine, provided your speakers stay near the vase! To solve this problem you need an assistant and a following mic.

The mic can be secured in a variety

of mountings. A pistol grip is one; this is a handgrip with a shock-absorbing cradle for the mic, enabling it to be pointed towards the speakers and follow movements without the rattles which usually comes from lashing a mic to a fixture. Keeping out of vision, by crawling underneath the shot, moving forward of the camera to the side of the shot or climbing above the shot, working with the arm comfortably extended, it is possible to keep the mic close to the sources (under one metre) whilst covering action two or three metres away from camera.

The other method of following action is with the telescopic microphone pole, or fish-pole, often erroneously called a boom. It is possible to improvise one using any wooden or metal pole. Use the shortest length necessary; it may help if you weight the end furthest from the mic as a counterbalance. Fix the mic so that it is angled but points forward of the pole and check that it does not pick up any noise from insecure fixing, your handling of the pole or from the cable rattling against it. Whether it is extended above or below the shot, one hand should hold the pole at the counterbalance point and act as fulcrum, the other should then be used to guide the mic. You will find that its length and weight will limit the time it can be used!

An improvised fishpole – a personal mic taped to a cane.

Checking a mic position – a fishpole with directional mic.

PLACING MICS

- Whenever possible use one mic for each sound source.
- Use directional mics for preference. The exceptions are when recording non-directional ambient sounds or when the mic can be placed much closer to the required sound than the background sound.
- Position mics as close to sound sources as practicable.
- Aim it at the mouth – no other part of the anatomy speaks!
- In locations with high background noise, position speakers so that aiming the mic at them points it away from unwanted sound.
- Mics can be put on stands, slung from ceilings, clamped to boards or walls or clipped or pinned to people's clothing but they always should be fixed securely so that there are no distracting bumps or rattles.

Three questions decide whether the mic should be above, below or at the side of the shot:

- Where can you get closest?
- In which direction is the speaker looking?
- Which direction will reject unwanted sounds and give the best sound uncoloured by the surrounding acoustic?

Two possible problems are:

- Sometimes pointing the mic down may get closest to the sound source but not enough to avoid picking up unwanted reflected sound from a marble or concrete floor.
- Pointing up may seem best because the speaker's head may droop, but you could get reverberations from a high, church-type ceiling or roof.

CABLES AND ADAPTORS

Using separate mics and mixers means paying attention to cables. The weak link of a sound system is its joins – the plugs and sockets. Never introduce uncertainties into your sound setups; avoid using 'adaptors' for cables and use the right components.

SOUND MIXING

Sound needs mixing whenever more than one mic is being used. Mixers give control of recording levels (loudness) from each mic separately and blends them to achieve maximum clarity without distortion. Some mixers have extra controls to adjust the character of the sound, increasing or decreasing the bass, the high frequencies or the mid-range. This is useful to filter out such unwanted sounds as the deep rumble of traffic, without affecting the main voice frequencies.

Mixers also allow you to use the nearest or most appropriate of your mics when you need them; this is useful if the subject is moving around the location or setting and you do not have a 'following' mic.

Sound mixers are best used with recorders with a manual control setting, although they may help combine mics in good balance for recorders with AGC (*see* Glossary).

SETTING A LEVEL

Having positioned your mic first make sure it is connected! Then check that the volume or level controls for each channel on the mixer are at zero.

Ask the speaker or musician for each mic to speak or play in the manner, and at the level, they intend for the recording. Raise the fader for that channel on the mixer until the level indicator points to (or 'peaks' at) the maximum signal level recommended by the equipment instructions. When you have established this peak take the control down a little to cope with the unexpected! MARK THE FADER POSITION ON THE EQUIPMENT with an erasable pen or pencil.

When you have set each channel separately you are then able to fade them up whenever you need them, singly or in groups, to the preset positions. Do not have mics 'open' when they are not needed – they will only hear unwanted noises.

Use the main or master fader to control levels at the beginning and end of the recording, fading up from silence with the first picture and fading out to silence as the last picture fades. Listen and watch the level indicators all the time, making slight adjustments if necessary. Avoid abrupt changes.

Remember:

that your aim is to record only the speech, music and sounds necessary for your video, eliminating everything else. The soundtrack should be clear, in perspective with the pictures (close shots should have close sound, long shots less close) and in character with the video you wish to make.

FINALLY, SOUND CLARITY DEPENDS ON:

- Using the correct type of mic.
- Placing it close to the sound source you want and as far away from the sounds you do not want to hear.
- Recording at the correct signal level.

LIGHTING

In general, colour TV pictures look good when there is a fairly low contrast ratio within them. This means that illumination should be evenly spread with soft shadows.

Bright, cloudy days provide the best natural light; shaded areas on sunny days can provide good light for close-ups and interviews. If you have to work in sunlight try to avoid people having to face the sun. Good results can be obtained by placing your subjects with their backs to the sun and lighting the face with a reflector. Reflecting surfaces can be used to direct daylight to shaded areas and indoors, as well as reflecting artificial light.

Working indoors imposes one main problem on lighting – providing enough. This need not mean having sophisticated video lamps; instead, simply turn on lots of domestic lights. Their strength can be increased by using higher wattage bulbs.

Whichever type of light you use avoid shining it directly on to your subjects; instead diffuse it or reflect it. Fortunately, most homes have a good surface for doing both, namely, the white ceiling.

To light your indoor picture set up the camera shot and if you do not have a large size colour viewfinder, feed the picture to a TV screen or monitor. Shine the most powerful lamps you have on the white ceiling so that they reflect down on the areas you wish to light – the subject and the background. Ensure that the lamp lighting the subject is behind and to the side of the camera.

Check that:

- The illumination gives one soft shadow which makes a pleasing shape to the subject's face.
- The light is falling on the front of the face and not the top of the head.
- The eyes are lit and there are no dark shadows under them.

Although your camcorder will produce some sort of image in low light conditions it is best to increase the light or lamps until there is sufficient for a good picture. Low light pictures do not copy or edit well.

Tips to try

Ensuring that your camcorder has enough light to produce a technically good picture requires specialist knowledge and test equipment but looking at a good monitor or TV screen can provide a valuable guide.

- Ensure that the camera is set to normal and not 'low light'.
- Frame and light the shot.
- See how much depth of focus you have; is it easy to focus manually or is finding focus very critical?
- See how 'firm' are the dark areas; are they definitely dark or 'noisy' (grey-dark, with fuzzy dancing grain appearing)?
- Video pictures with adequate light have definite, firm dark areas and good depth of focus.

Beware – continually check if the camcorder record button is ON or OFF. It is very easy to get out of sync with these controls and shoot hours of fuzzy tape with nothing of the action you wanted!

Indoors using a reflector to light the faces.

You may not always want a microphone in shot.

A shaded area providing soft pleasing light on the faces.

Section 5 **Telling a Story**

For other people to enjoy your videos they need to tell a definite story. This section shows you how to do this, advising on what to include or exclude, helping you to list the main actions and showing you how to avoid being sidetracked. It also has tips on planning ahead and for thinking on your feet, helping you make the best of your expertise.

To help us communicate accurately and efficiently writers and readers follow an agreed grammar. Film and video makers have done the same. There are agreed structures and punctuation points – knowing them frees you to show what you mean, mean what you show and yet still have creative fun.

Think of it this way: to tell your video story shots are sentences, scenes are paragraphs and sequences are chapters. The simile does not stretch much further except to say that, just as in a written language, a cut, a mix and a fade down or up, are all devices which have agreed uses. Misuse them and the confusion caused will destroy the meaning of your story.

Use the word 'scene' to mean a clearly defined part of the action (which will be divided into shots) and use the word 'sequence' to mean a series of scenes comprising a defined section of your story.

THE LANGUAGE OF SHOTS
The pictures, or shots, taken of people are described in camera language in relation to the length of the human body shown. All shots are presumed to include the head.

- A Long shot (LS) shows the whole body from head to feet.
- A Medium shot (MS) shows the body from head to waist.
- A Medium close-up (MCu) shows the body from head to mid chest.
- A Close-up (CU) shows the head and shoulders only. Close-up may also be used to describe a shot which isolates either a specifically described part of the body (eg, feet or hands), part of a large object (eg, a piano keyboard), or the whole of a small object (eg, a book or a telephone).
- A Big Close-up (BCu) is sometimes called for, this concentrates on the

Long shot (LS).

Medium Close-up (MCu).

Close-up (CU).

Wide Angle (W/A) .

eyes and includes as much of the rest of the face as is required.
- A Wide angle (W/A) does not relate to the human body but should include the entire setting or area of action. This type of shot is sometimes misdescribed as a Very Long shot.

THE LANGUAGE OF PICTURE CHANGES
Having chosen a shot to convey the most meaning there will come a point where it no longer serves its purpose and you change it for another. The type of change could be a cut, a mix or a fade.

A **cut** is the instantaneous change of one shot for another. It is the equivalent of flicking the eyes from one place to another, the change being imperceptible. Cuts are made in only three circumstances (whether you edit in-camera or later): on A LOOK, a MOVE or a WORD (or sound like a musical beat). All good editing follows these rules and it is part of a director or cameraman's job to look for those moments and clarify them during the shooting if necessary.

Never cut between shots of the same or similar size of the same subject, even if they are from different angles. It is an unnatural eye movement and always looks like a mistake. A good cut is unseen; it does not interrupt the flow of a scene but establishes a rhythm to propel it forward, each shot the necessary outcome of the one before it.

The cut on a look: this may be a head turn or a movement of the eyes but because it calls attention to something outside the frame the viewer wishes to see it.

The cut on a move: again the viewer's attention is directed outside the frame, perhaps by a gesture – the arm pointing and the eye wishing to follow. It may be a walk or a rise, the subject carries our attention beyond the frame and the viewer wants to follow the action.

The cut on the word: if a question is asked we wish to see the reply, if a statement is made we wish to see its effect. The same would be true of some sounds – a bell ringing, an explosion; just as our bodies move to music what could be more natural than cutting a shot with the musical beat?

A **mix** is the fading out of one picture

and the simultaneous fading in of another. Use it to indicate a lapse of time within a scene or to get from one scene to another where there is a possible time lapse, or in getting to and from captions. Wrongly used it is simply a dirty cut, indicating that you have been unable to find the correct picture change.

A **fade in /fade out** means fading a picture in from or to black. Usually used to begin or end a scene or sequence, use it in a similar way as the mix but to indicate a longer time lapse.

Wipes (vertical, horizontal, diagonal) can be used to replace one image by another using lines or shapes travelling across the screen. These have no agreed meanings but are a decorative method of changing pictures. In most video stories it is difficult to find an appropriate use for them; if you want to use them, do so sparingly since they call attention to your editing techniques. They have a place in pop videos , for example, where the visuals are the content. Too often they are used to distract the audience from poor shooting, absence of craft and lack of content.

[For more on editing *see* also section The Final Polish].

DECIDING CAMERA POSITIONS

The picture (or shot) you see from a camera can be classified as either 'objective' or 'subjective'.

For an objective shot the camera is placed so that you see the scene from outside the action – the view is that of a spectator, not a participant. This type of shot is needed at some point within any sequence so that the viewer can see the position and relationship of everything within the scene. It is often described as a Wide-angle or Establishing Shot. However, because it is essentially a spectator's view its dramatic effect can be to distance the viewer, preventing any impression of involvement.

For a subjective shot the camera is positioned to give the impression that you are seeing the action, or an object, from the viewpoint of someone involved within the scene or action.

The type of subjective shot used – long, medium, close-up, from above, below or moving – will be dictated by the actual proximity of the subjects, the need the audience has to see more clearly or be more closely involved, or, if it is a drama, the emotional state of the characters. Thus, if A and B have been seen as people of equal height, standing

closely together, it is obvious that the subjective shot of A – supposedly from B's viewpoint – could not be a low angle long shot!

Avoid taking shots of the same subject which immediately follow each other in the action from the same angle and never at the same length.

Try always to place your camera ahead of the action so that movements approach the audience. Movements to the side of the frame or away from the camera hold the attention less.

When choosing a camera position ensure that it does not cross 'the line'. This imaginary line runs between either of the sides of the setting as it has been established on-camera or between the characters or performers in the action, again as they have been established on-camera. If all camera positions are kept to the same side of it people actually looking at each other will be shown so if a camera shoots from the far side of it people actually looking at each other will not seem to do so when the shots are edited together.

COVERING THE ACTION

People meet, perform some actions and talk, then part.

This simple statement describes the basis of any video scene or action. eg.

Keep camera position angles complementary

the interview situation, but how do you shoot it?

Narrative Shots
Firstly, you must cover the action; your audience will expect to see and hear the people meet, go through their actions, talk and part. These pictures tell us what is going on and are often called narrative shots. Unless it is a drama, such shots will be objective; we are not yet invited to become part of the action – simply to follow it. Consequently the pictures will need to show the relationship of the people to each other and their setting, and will tend to be wide angles or long shots.

Subjective Shots
However, our script says that after meeting the people perform some actions; if the camera is to be like us it will want to see exactly what is going on. So from now on the shots must be closer, to concentrate on the actions and exclude things that are already known, such as the setting or the exact number of people present. These shots are also likely to be taken from different angles than the narrative shots, not only because we need to see better, but because we need to understand what these events look like to those involved. And if the actions express some conflict, the shots will have become subjective.

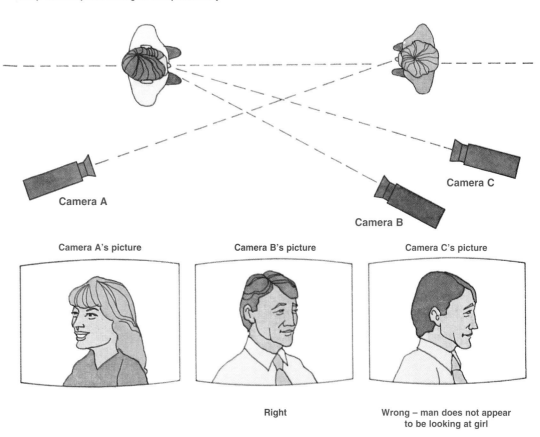

Camera A

Camera B

Camera C

Camera A's picture

Camera B's picture

Camera C's picture

Right

Wrong – man does not appear to be looking at girl

Complementary Close-ups

And now the people talk to each other. Apart from needing to hear clearly what they say, the camera again follows human behaviour – we would not simply want to see who is talking but look into their faces, their eyes especially, to assess the truth and sincerity of what they are saying. Thus, we not only have subjective shots (each speaker seen from the other's point of view) but complementary close-ups. This is not only necessary in drama, but is also the visual structure of all interviews.

Cutaways

As long as we follow the pattern of talk with our visuals, these shots are narrative, too. After a time, when we know this pattern, we may need extra information to supplement or confirm the verbal discussion. As we are dealing with a visual medium we should demonstrate and the way to do this is with extra shots. Cutaway from the established locale to show pictures from any source which is relevant.

LAST SHOTS

The consequence of our analysis has taken the camera closer and closer to what is happening. How do we end? Must we go back to a wide shot? To arrive at a conclusion we must always ask what is the truth of the story? Our script says simply 'they part'; what is the best way to express that in the video language?

If an interviewer says:, "We must end there for the moment", that is all we need to know; we do not need to see the people put on their hats and coats and catch the train. The end is marked with a punctuation point, a group shot and a fade out. The same principle applies at the end of most ceremonies – a wedding or the State Opening of Parliament; the real action finishes before the polite handshakes. Those punctuation points have no relevance for us so they can can omitted. So, if in our example the two people are in a drama and have finished their talk with a kiss in close-up, all that may be needed is a continuation of the close-up long enough to see their heads part. Alternatively, perhaps the talk has been angry and the decision to part has been spoken by one character, the story may then best be told by holding on his shot as he stalks away. Or it may be more relevant to see the other person's reaction as he or she watches the

departure. A good general principle for ending a scene is – do not prolong it and do not change the shot unless there is something else to show.

MORE ON SUBJECTIVE SHOTS

Subjective shots are important in drama but they are also the basis for shooting all interviews. They have a set of rules all of their own to make them credible.

Shots of people talking or reacting to each other should match; that is they should be of the same size, with the same headroom and at complementary angles. Matching the head size of the two shots makes us believe that the people are talking to each other; if one is in medium shot and the other close, the

effect is to make us think that one person has moved away.

Also match the headroom and eye-height within the frame (mark their positions in the viewfinder with a chinagraph pencil).

For both camera positions the angles of acceptance of the the lenses should be the same. Any variation could produce different types of picture (depth of focus, sense of compression, contrast ratios).

Ensure lens heights and camera positions are complimentary. Draw an imaginary line drawn between the participants at eye level, the lens heights should be set along that line (so that with people of different heights the shot of the taller should be from below, the shorter from above). The same for the horizontal

Different angles may be either objective (the action observed) or subjective (the action seen from a character's viewpoint).

Equally, this low angle could be chosen as a subjective shot or as a dramatic narrative shot.

plane – the camera positions should deviate from the line by the same angle.

THE SENSE OF DIRECTION

In scripts or speech when describing shots, action or the placing of people or objects the accepted convention is to refer to camera right or left, things as seen looking from the camera position to the subject.

Whether you are shooting dramatized scenes or not, do not confuse your viewers by muddling their sense of direction. Just as you ensure the direction of every look and move within a location will be correct by avoiding crossing the line with the camera, so it is important to plan the rights and lefts of material shot on a series of locations.

If from an aerial shot we see two armies moving towards each other, one from the left the other from the right, the most positive way we can identify which group is which (when we cut closer to watch them ford a river, say), is their direction of travel. In the aerial shot those we saw on the right moving towards the left must always be shown moving from right to left and vice versa. This idea holds good for other situations.

If one group of people or objects is consistently shown moving towards camera from right to left across the frame and other groups are shown moving towards camera from left to right, the suggestion is that they must eventually meet. But if the second group is shown travelling left to right away from camera the suggestion is that they will miss each other. Again, if the Lord Mayor's processional car is always shown travelling left to right then we know he is making progress. If it suddenly appears travelling right to left the viewer cannot be sure that he has not turned back. And if you were to show the following procession as travelling in a different direction to the leading car, depending on whether they were shown approaching or receding, you would suggest either that a head-on collision was coming – or that they had lost each other! *Keeping directions constant avoids confusing the viewer.*

SHOOTING SOUND

Try to record the best sound you can especially in interviews and commentaries where the speaker may not be seen on screen and you cannot

ABOVE LEFT and RIGHT
For drama or interviews, shots should match.

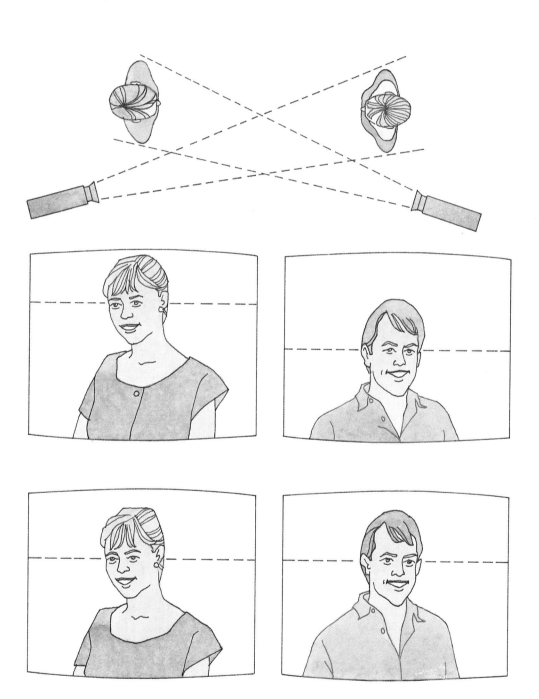

Match headroom and eye height.

35

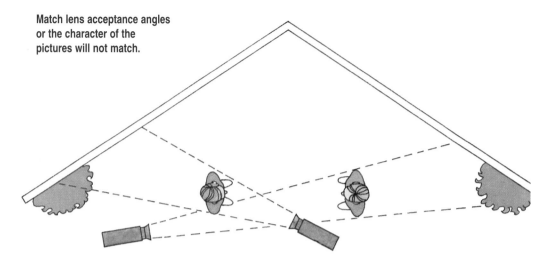

Match lens acceptance angles or the character of the pictures will not match.

The telephoto lens fills the background with the bush and keeps it out of focus.

The wide angle lens used makes the background bush small and clear.

use your eyes to help you understand what is being said.

There are three types of sound which can be very helpful to the final result and which need to be recorded specially – wildtrack, sound effects and dialogue for post-synching.

WILDTRACK

This is the background sound of the scenes you shoot. When you piece together your shots you will find that, even though they may all have been recorded on the same location, the level and type of sound is different. At the start of one shot you have caught the sound of an aeroplane receding; as it ends a lorry is revving-up and is cut off abruptly. The next shot starts quietly so calls attention to the abrupt end of the previous one. As it continues you hear some distant dogs bark which are cut off sharply as the shot cuts, and so on. To smooth all this out you need to record a wildtrack – that is, an unsynchronized recording of a continuous background long enough to cover the final sequence. Although it is a sound only recording use your camera for this (preferably with an external, plug-in microphone); if you

are editing in-camera, this sound-only recording must be on a separate tape. [*See* section The Final Polish on how to use wildtrack in your completed programme.]

Keep angles complementary.

Camera A   Camera B   Camera C

Right, sees girl from man's eye level.

Camera B, right sees man from girl's eye level.

Camera C, wrong, although le_ at man's eye height he does not appear to look at the girl

SOUND EFFECTS

Even though your shots of animals, machines and other noise-making subjects may have the noise they make recorded synchronously on the shots, it is possible they will give you the same variations of level and quality as the backgrounds. Record them separately to be used later in the same way as wildtracks.

POST-SYNC DIALOGUE

There are times when you find a stunning wide angle shot and you want to put someone in it talking either to camera or to a second person. The problem is how can you record the sound? The shot is too wide for the camera microphone to pick up the sound and it is generally impractical to have a 30-metre roll of mic cable in your holiday kit. A radio microphone could be one answer; however, if you want to hear the second person clearly it is not the complete answer. You could also record a commentary when you get home but that may not capture the atmosphere. A possible answer is to record the dialogue on site but post-sync it.

The first thing to remember is that whatever the duration of the wide angle shot you will not want to hold it for long after the speech starts; after the eye has taken in the situation your audience will want to see the speakers more clearly. Consequently you may only need to plan how to cover 20 or 30 seconds of speech.

So firstly, get your performers to agree or memorize exactly what they will say. Rehearse it to set the timing, then record the wide shot with your participant(s) far enough away from camera (possibly with them moving) so that lips cannot be clearly seen. Now record the dialogue whilst you are still on the location but with the mic close enough to give clear sound. If you are editing in-camera, this should be a sound-only recording on a separate tape; if you are editing later you could shoot it as the first part of a two-shot intended to cut onto the end of the wide angle.

THINKING AHEAD

Having encountered the language of video it is time to apply it.

However well we speak a language we never speak in public or write a letter without thinking first what we want to say and what the impact might be – so why should making a video be any different.

Here is a plan for your video/letter

Say in a sentence why you are making this particular video (eg, to show my friends the sort of holiday we had; to show my parents what their grandchild looks like and that he/she is intelligent and happy; to impress my sister and her family in Australia with what we achieved for charity at the annual village show).

Taking the village show as our example, first list the possible things you could record (get from the organizers a running order of events plus information on other attractions).

Do a 'recce' (reconnaissance visit) to all the locations which are essential to the story and with which you are not familiar.

Analyze your list in the light of the knowledge of the location:

- Are they actions which would make a scene?
- Is the idea best represented by a person you could interview?
- Is it an object which would go into a scene?

Exclude all the ideas which do not fit in with the reason you are making the video.

Exclude sections which make the same point twice.

Put what is left into an order which tells a story (eg, the preparations for the show, the day's highlights in chronological order, the results of the show – any benefits?). This is your running order.

Decide the length of your video (up to 15 minutes should not test the patience of your friends) and the length of each of the sections. In this way you keep control of your shooting and of the overall shape of the finished result.

Decide the pace of the sections –which should be fast and which slow. The variation in the pace of events will help you keep your viewer's attention. If you have more than two slow sections next to each other, change the running order.

Decide the type of shots and sound needed for each section. Will you need to borrow, hire or make anything to record what you want? Will you need someone to help?

The (Imaginary) Line. Do not let your camera position cross the line.

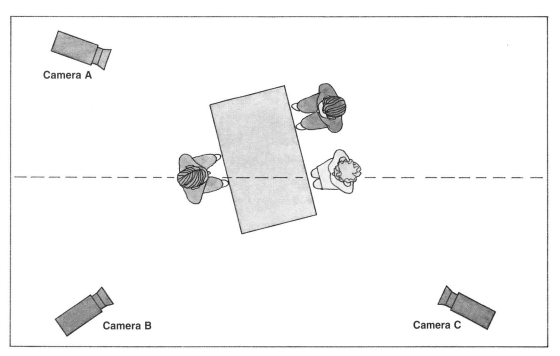

Camera A, wrong position has crossed the line.

Camera B, right.

Camera C, right.

Tell friends about the events around you – the Bloxtead Village Show.

EXAMPLE RUNNING ORDER
Bloxtead Village Show
1. **Opening** – teaser sequence to capture the flavour of the day – shots of children on rides and eating food.
30 secs
2. **Reason** for the show, plus statement about the family's involvement:
•Interview with Mrs Bloggs on (A) what they want to achieve during this year's Show and (B) as an end result.
1 min
•Interview Uncle Jim (on committee) to give family view.   2 mins
Both these should be recorded in the week before. Shoot cutaways for interviews as soon as possible.

3. **The Show:**   **Total: 8-9 mins**

Opening ceremony   30 secs
General shots, show size and type of event   45 secs
Children's races   1 min 30 secs

Crafts display   45 secs
Fast fairground rides   45 secs
Lunchtime food (variety sold and different eaters)   1 min
Vintage farm machinery display 1 min
Working animals competition   2 mins
Dusk shots   20 secs
Evening disco   30 secs

4. **The Results** – interview with Nurse Smith of Children's Hospital; she says how much was collected and how it will benefit the Children's Fund. Cutaways – monies being paid during the festival; exterior of hospital; interior, showing specific wards and machines if permission given.
1 - 2 mins
Last shot: Daughter Gillian, age 7, saying what she did on the day and what she thinks is the benefit of the Children's Fund.   20-30 secs

Total Running Time: 12 mins 30 secs

This running order illustrates that giving a portion of time to each section means you have to think how important it is in comparison to the whole. Also, when you see that the children's races are to fill 1 minute 30 seconds and that the average shot length in most productions is eight seconds then you realize that you need only shoot 11 or 12 shots, maximum. If you are editing in-camera, such planning helps keep tight control of both the pace and the overall running time. If you are to edit later it helps you not to overshoot.
Use this checklist to make decisions:
• Does any section need extra equipment?
• Does any section need extra help?
• Is any permission needed to shoot any section?
• Do you need to do a recce for any section?
• Does anyone need to be briefed beforehand, if only as a courtesy (it may get you extra facilities on-site).

STARTING TO ROLL

Some people just like to keep the camera running, diligently following the action - and perhaps the inaction – as it unfolds; these are practitioners of the developing shot, sometimes called the Long Take. To do this well usually requires years of experience and no little artifice. To hold one shot without cutting means that the picture and the action within it must be constantly interesting. Over the past 100 years of moving image production there have been a few, and famous, examples of the successful long take and their one consistent common denominator is the time it has taken to prepare them – usually many days. For lesser creative mortals, and those without Hollywood-size budgets and time, it means mastering the art of cutting and editing.

EDITING AS YOU SHOOT

For most people the making of a video with all the things they want to see, done with a sense of style and changes of pace and interest, means creating it in the camera as they go along. To do this successfully means thinking clearly and thinking ahead.

It also means knowing the techniques for telling your story – the language of shots, moves and editing. It means shooting the minimum you need. And it also means reviewing sequences as you shoot them since you only have the one chance to record over the whole or part of an overlong or unsuccessful sequence, before you shoot another one!

Look for good cutaways.

Show the craft displays.

Fairground rides.

Decide before you shoot:
- What you want to show.
- How long the video should be.
- How you intend to divide up the time.
- The outline shape of each segment or sequence.

Actually, it is possible to make some adjustments afterwards to the material you have shot but the opportunities are limited. [Look at section The Final Polish.]

TO EDIT IN CAMERA.
1. Assess the situation you are about to shoot and try to decide how long it should run, or roughly how many shots it is worth. (Then, until you have gained experience, discipline yourself to record just over half your original estimate!)

Lunch break.

shooting extra sound, special effects or noises and particularly the background atmosphere of the location, Wildtrack, to cover shots with low (or no) appropriate backgrounds.

Whatever your method, the end result should be the recording of enough audio and picture to offer choices during editing.

SHOOTING TO EDIT

1. Think how you might want the scene to look. Assess how many angles you want to see the action from and the appropriate cutting rate. Estimate whether you want to keep all of the action or only parts of it.

2. If the action cannot be repeated, shoot it from a position and in a way that

2. Decide a shape for the scene, preferably knowing what sort of shot you will open and close with.

3. Learn to cut on cutting points.

4. Shoot as the action starts, not before (or after).

5. Cut as the action stops or, if the action is not prearranged, the moment you realize there is enough to indicate what the shot is about.

6. Alternatively, stop your camera when you are sure you have enough material. Review it. Stop or Pause on the cutting point – whichever system your camera has to allow you a clean recording start without picture disturbance. If you have time, this procedure allows you to cut super-fluous material and also choose the edit point with greater accuracy.

7. Do not overshoot. Be tough with yourself, stop the moment that part of the story is told.

SHOOTING TO EDIT AFTERWARDS
If you are able to edit your material afterwards you still need to know and make decisions on the points already listed but you are able to postpone final decisions on the best of the recorded material. Your foremost thought in shooting for editing should be coverage. It may mean shooting the same action twice from different angles. It may mean shooting alternative pictures to the main action so that your story can be told in the faces, actions and reactions of those not immediately involved. And it may mean

Look for good cutaways.

Vintage farm machinery.

40

will allow you to record it all without breaks.

3. If it can be repeated you may wish to divide it into sections, shooting each section more than once, but each time from a different viewpoint and possibly shot length.

4. Shoot reaction shots and cutaways.

5. Shoot wildtrack.

6. To ensure stable edits, always run the camera for 10 seconds before and after the action you intend to use.

7. Be guided by professional practice, keep your shooting ratio between seven and 10 to one (depending on the style of production). This means that for every minute of finished screen time aim to shoot between seven and 10 minutes – and that includes all marking boards and run up times.

8. Mark your shots. Write a shot number or brief message for yourself on child's slate or with a felt tip pen on scrap paper. Shoot it filling the screen at the beginning of each shot or take. It will save hours of time when you are trying to find shots later.

9. Use short reels, an hour maximum. Again, this is to save time in editing. Finding the one shot you need when it is recorded two hours and 23 minutes in to a three hour tape is no fun – especially if you need to do that sort of search several times within an hour!

The animal competitions.

End with the dusk shots.

Section 6 Weddings

Making a good recording of a wedding involves just about every possible video-making skill. To avoid disappointing friends and relatives, who can be very unforgiving in this instance, undertake it only when you are well practised in these three areas – technical recording skills, story-telling and detailed planning

Weddings are a combination of ceremony and ritual coupled with informal and uninhibited moments. They demand the programme-making skills associated with the best outside broadcasts and documentaries, not to mention those of news-gathering!

Basically, there are always three elements. First, the preparations, which give the video-maker the chance to put what follows into a family or community context and make a dramatic build-up. Then there is the ceremony or ritual, in which the couple express their change of status before their priest or elders and their family or community; this is the section for richness and colour. And finally, there is the celebration – a release of tension and the happy ending. Whether it is to be a religious or civic ceremony or one solemnized with a traditional ritual, the patterns have similarities. The video-making ideas explored here can be applied in many contexts.

The ideas are also explained at various levels of complexity. You may enjoy co-operating with a group of friends to undertake a full-scale documentary, or it may be that simpler methods are indicated. The best advice for those making a video with one camera without help is to make a short, highlights-type programme.

Running Order
NB – the term church is used to cover any place in which the ceremony will be held. If two cameras are in use the coverage has been split between A and B.

Action	Location(s)
Opening sequence	Optional
Preparations	Bride's home (A) Groom's home (B) Inside the church (B) Reception/party venue (A or B)

Bride's departure	Bride's home (A)
Guests arriving at church	Outside/Inside church (B)
Bride's arrival at church	Outside/Inside church (A + B)
The ceremony, (must include: organ music at start, vows, exchange of rings, signing register).	Inside church (A + B)
The photographs, plus any post-ceremony activity and then the departure of couple.	Outside church (A)
Arrivals at reception /party	Reception venue (B)
Speeches Cake cutting Dancing and revelry	Reception venue (A later)
Final shot	From church or outside reception.

If you have been asked to record the wedding, ensure that you have an agreed running time; it will condition everything you do. A half-hour highlights programme obviously requires much less in the way of facilities than a two hour epic. Whatever the running time, however, plan in great detail.

Recce all the locations, even if you know them well. Unless you make videos everyday you will never have noticed all the details you now need to master (eg, if it is a sunny day, from which direction does the light come and

ABOVE
Build up to the ceremony with shots of the preparations.

BELOW
Get ahead to record the bride's arrival for the ceremony.

LEFT
At Registry Offices the ante-room can provide extra shots.

what does it shine on at the time of the ceremony, where are the mains plugs, and what type are they – at the bride's house and reception venue if different?).

List the technical facilities; will you need: one, two (or three) cameras? Tripods? A dolly? How many mics and of what type? Will you need lights? Spare bulbs? How much camera, sound or mains cable? Adaptors? Battery belt?

Have you a video location tool-kit? How much tape? Which method of editing will be used? What transport and other assistance do you need and can you get?

Get clearances and permissions. Will you be allowed to record in the locations and from the exact positions you want? Do they have electricity supplies or other facilities you can use?

Do any of the musicians know you intend to record them? Do not assume that all of the people involved will be happy to give unconditional consent for your shooting.

Where is the parking?

Work through the running order in detail to decide the duration and shape of each sequence.

Annotated
Wedding – Outline Script
Total programme running time – 45 mins

Opening 2 mins
This can be as creative as you and your friends wish. It may include stills from the bride and groom's photo albums showing them at different stages in their lives or simply during courting. You may wish to interview bride and groom separately some days before the wedding on how they met, their impressions of each other, their feelings about the ceremony, etc. The two could be cut together as a run up to a shot of the church exterior (music in the background) with the date superimposed.

Preparations up to bride leaving for church 6 mins
Use a documentary approach to capture the real atmosphere – as with any sequence, it must tell a clearly defined part of the story. Depending on what you find, it can be one or two narrative shots with cutaways or all brief shots, very impressionistic to convey speed and detail. If all is calm and ordered show it that way; do not impose a clichéd approach. Get shots of mother and father (ask him if he will preview his speech from memory!), the bridesmaids, flowers and finally the bride as the finishing touches are put to the dress. Possibly, use cross-cutting to the groom's preparations both for contrast and pace.

First choice lighting should be daylight but if it is too directional indoors, giving dark sides to faces, use a reflector. If it is not strong enough, put on the house lights, replacing the ordinary bulbs with high wattage ones. Otherwise use a strong video light reflected from the ceiling and powered from the mains. Use a battery-powered video lamp shining directly on the subject as a last resort (this type of light runs batteries down fast and unless used very carefully is not at all flattering).

Use shots of any preparations in church or at the reception to help build suspense – simple actions like preparing the cake or laying the tables. Shoot fast and slow movements, however familiar, to enable you to point up contrasts when the material is intercut.

Watch for lefts and rights. You may like to show the bride as always looking and moving left to right, and the groom from right to left until they finally meet in church. This would mean

planing the directions dependent on how you are able to shoot the bride leaving for the church in her car.

Guests arriving at church   2 mins
Shoot from outside to use daylight (position the camera in the porch if it is raining). The running time allows you to show about 12 arrivals. To avoid overshooting pre-select those to be recorded and ensure that you – or a helper – can identify them later. Do not vary the camera position much but vary the length of shot to make editing easier. Possibly you could pre-record the organ music and start it behind these shots.

So far you will have been using a news/documentary approach to shooting and could use a mic attached to the camera. The exception would be for the interviews. If you can

cope, use hand or rifle mics, if not, ensure that the speakers are close enough to the camera to be well within range of the attached mic.

Bride's arrival, exit from car, entry into church   1 min.
Continue organ music under this, keeping a believable sound perspective. At the car the music would be distant, well down into the traffic, increasing as the bride gets closer to the church and dominating as she is seen inside. Back-time it to end at a point when she is walking down the aisle or arriving at the altar steps.

(The Back-timing method – time the music, then, when the picture sequence is complete, note the time where you wish the music to finish. Run the tape back for the exact duration of the music

– by starting your transfer of the music at that point it will end at the selected time.)

The Ceremony, including the signing of the Register   15 mins
In situations where the ceremony cannot be recorded, as in UK Registrar's Offices, you may care to substitute a shot of the building or a symbolic picture with a few words of appropriate commentary. In the case of ceremonies conducted by Registrars it is generally possible to resume the coverage as the couple sign the Register.

Whatever the faith or type of ceremony, use the following ideas on which to arrange your shooting.

First, identify the main participants. They will be the couple and the celebrant (a priest or in some ceremonies a family member). Thus your camera positions

will need to be in the right places to capture the interaction between the couple and the celebrant. The community (family or congregation) although important, is secondary.

Then select the main camera position. This should be of the couple from their front, usually shot from behind and to one side of the priest. It will also need to be far enough to the side so that her/his movements do not block the shot. Choose the side which favours the bride and try to ensure that the position is a good working distance from the couple. It should allow a long shot of them with the zoom at its widest. Avoid working closer. The position could be more distant, but not so far that you would have difficulty in holding steady close-ups of the couple. From this position you should be able to get a variety of shots of them and also wide shots and close-ups of the congregation. In buildings with a gallery, do not be tempted to shoot from

above – closer shots will only show tops of heads.

The camera must be on a tripod. If the surface and available space permit, a set of rolling wheels for the tripod would be invaluable to allow sideways adjustments to the shots, especially if you have to cover a lectern position. Next, consider the mics; do not attempt to use the attached camera mic as nothing will be in range. Try to get permission to sling (hang) a mic just above the heads of bride, groom and priest; if you use a cardioid – one side to the priest, the other to the couple – it would probably pick up the congregation's singing as well; otherwise an omni-directional mic could be tried, unless there is a lot of traffic noise.

If you cannot sling a mic put it on a stand between the priest and couple. As it is unlikely to pick up the congregation you may need a second mic for them which might also pick up the sound

of the organ or choir if they are facing its direction. If not, you will need a third mic to pick up the music. Should the priest give an address from another position – say a lectern – mic that. Alternatively, fit the priest with a radio mic.

Aim to get all mics within one metre of the individual speakers' mouths. For instrumentalists and choirs try to get a rehearsal; their mic(s) should be placed far enough away to get the full range of their sound with clarity, yet close enough to minimize any building acoustic and background noise.

Especially if there is only one camera covering the ceremony, and you intend to edit, use a good quality audio recorder to make a continuous soundtrack. This allows you times to reposition the camera and when you come to edit you have a better choice of material. You could use the appropriate sections edited in-camera plus sections where you lay down pictures and sound separately. (*See* section The Final Polish: Insert Editing.)

Finally, must you use extra light? You may need to take the camera into the building on a dull day to make an assessment. Daylight is the preferred illumination; you may have colour balance problems mixing day with artificial light. With dark buildings in winter, you will obviously need to explore alternatives. Can any of the existing lights be moved to light the bride and groom? The best position would be above the camera and within an arc of 35 degrees to the right of a line between the camera and the couple; it should not need to tilt down more than 35 degrees from the horizontal. Otherwise, if you can bring in a two kilowatt lamp, position it here. Any other available lamps could be used to cross light the couple (shining on them from the far side of the priest to fill in shadows but ensure the power is below that of the main light), to light the couple from behind (thus also lighting the priest), lighting the lectern shot and lastly, the congregation. In other words, light the close-up positions first and in order of importance.

Another camera on the shoot gives great possibilities. If you look back at the Running Order you will see that locations have the letter A or B; this is a suggested division of the shoot between two cameras. Before the ceremony, use the second camera for coverage of the bride's preparations, allowing the main camera to cover the groom or reception shots and get to the church interior first. Also, use the second camera to cover the bride to the moment she comes down the aisle; during the ceremony, keep it mobile to pick up shots from behind the congregation of the whole scene, the priest's address, plus any cutaways and close-ups from the 'camera side'. Ensure that it does not cross the line and also ensure that both cameras shoot their cutaways and reaction shots with people looking in the right direction (the priest should be looking right to left, everyone else left to right).

If you use more than one camera, plan to coordinate shot changes. For example, if the priest gives an address, especially from a lectern on the 'camera side', arrange it so that as (s)he walks out of the main shot position, the second camera will reposition early enough to let her/him walk in to a mid shot at the lectern. The start of the address could then be a signal to the main camera to change to another position to shoot a series of cutaways, particularly to cover edits in the address (beware of crossing the line). As the address ends the main camera resumes coverage of the bride and groom and the moment the priest leaves the lectern shot, camera two resumes taking cutaways. At the end of the ceremony it could take a wide shot whilst the main camera repositions for the register shots or vice-versa.

Whilst the register is being signed the free camera repositions to cover the lighter moments of the taking of the official photos. It may go on to cover the couple's departure or the free camera could do this, depending on the geography and the timing of the reception.

The photographs and departure of the couple   3 mins

This is documentary-style shooting. Show the overall situation but, having got the narrative shots of the family line-up or guests waiting for the couple, shoot cutaways which can give humour and character to the sequence (look for the elderly deep in conversation, the children in their best clothes, if not behaviour, relatives approving and disapproving).

The Reception/party-overall   15 mins

Arrivals   2 mins
Again, most of this is documentary-style coverage; the main concern will be to keep the shots level and steady. If there is to be a second guest-greeting sequence keep it brief, concentrating on MCus of the guests seen from over the bride or groom's shoulder. Use music to give a flow and cohesion to this brief segment and take one or two shots panning with guests, following them as they walk to their places. The best take could give you a transitional shot to the speeches sequence.

Speeches   5-6 mins
Use a tripod, you may need to record continuously for some time. Find a position in front of the speakers, turn around to the audience for reaction shots and cutaways. To ensure you hear the speeches use a mic on the table. If it is securely fixed to a short stand it can be placed in front of each speaker in turn – make arrangements to ensure it is! Since it is fairly certain that you will need to edit this sequence, record the sound on a good quality (reel-to-reel) audio recorder. During sections you suspect you will cut out – perhaps during introductions which you could do as commentary more briefly – turn the camera around to record the guests. Take various length shots of them listening,

Fade out on the dancing.

reacting and applauding. Edit the sequence cutting pictures and sound separately, the edited audio track should be used to make bridges between sections of sync speech; use cutaways to disguise cuts made to reduce length. For example, sections of the speeches may end with a joke; on the laugh line, edit in a shot of someone laughing, then start the sound of the next section under that shot, cut back to the speech. Skillfully done, few people will realize your abridgement.

If you have a second camera record the speeches in full, use the other camera for cutaways and reaction shots. Edit for length.

Ensure that there is enough light to see the speakers clearly. When planning your camera positions avoid a situation where the speakers have a window behind them. If necessary light the speakers.

Cake cutting   2 mins
This is hand-held stuff; tilt up or down for tall cakes to show the detail and get the moment of the cutting. Be alert on sound to catch any witty comments and be quick to pan off the couple at the right moment to get guest reaction, applause etc. Ask for retakes on cutting or reactions, if need be.

Couple's departure   2 mins
Start with an exterior wide shot of people waiting and prolong the suspense with closer shots. Cut wide as the couple emerge, pan them to their waiting vehicle and cut to MS as they enter it. Intercut couple and guests. Use a low or high angle as vehicle departs.

Dancing and revelry   2 mins
If there is a disco with strobe lights, cut to whatever impressionistic shots you can get under the circumstances. Use only as much as will convey the situation.

If it is ballroom-type dancing and you have enough light, collect as many humorous, characterful and light-hearted shots as possible. Edit as a picture sequence, dub music (not necessarily from the wedding) later.

The last shot might be the exterior of the reception venue with music fading, or a still frame from the ceremony (with music fading), or ....?

The cake cutting – check your tape and battery situation so that you do not miss it.

BUILDING A SEQUENCE FOR A HOLIDAY VIDEO

There are two main ingredients in your holiday video – you and what you saw and it is a good idea to have both represented in each section of the recording. You do not need many shots of yourself, but you should record a commentary (best done when you get home). Keep it very brief, using just a few words or phrases to amplify what is shown, giving either facts or your own reactions.

Shooting beach scenes is a tempting idea but one that is difficult to make successful. Take a brief sequence lasting one or two minutes observing people walking, talking or swimming, to convey an impression of the place. Or record your friends and family engaged in some activity – a sandcastle-building competition, beach football or cricket would all make lively sequences, while revealing the different characters in humorous ways.

Beware – camcorders are in danger on beaches. Heat, humidity, sea spray and sand quickly damage the mechanisms and tapes. and there is always the risk of theft.

IF YOU TAKE YOUR CAMCORDER ON THE BEACH:

- Shoot your material quickly and leave.
- If you cannot leave quickly, cover the camera to protect it from sand and sea spray. Keep it cool and do not leave it unguarded where it might be stolen.

CREATING SEQUENCES FOR YOUR HOLIDAY VIDEO

Here are two examples of creating a holiday sequence – one from a city – the other from the sea. First, London's famous Trafalgar Square with ideas of ways to shoot a sequence which should run for only a couple of minutes at the most.

THE CITY SCENE

1. Recall the last shot of the previous scene; perhaps you and your partner walking out of a shot in St James' Park. To start this sequence you need both a contrast to the last shot and something which announces where you are.

RIGHT

2. You could start on the top of a building and tilt down to discover you and/or your partner in the new location. In fact, you are almost spoilt for choice here; the top of St Martin's church, the dome of the National Gallery or Nelson on his column. The idea is that in one shot you have shown the change of location and placed yourself in it.

As soon as this point is made, cut to another shot, say a wide angle of the entire square. The commentary might continue or, better still, have some background music faded into the noise of the traffic and the square. This could continue throughout the sequence, tying all the shots together and making shots which have been held too long seem the right duration.

LEFT

3. Depending on what you find of interest, cut to any closer shots from the wide angle. Perhaps after a couple of five second shots you would want to show yourselves walking through the square. Two points here: first place the camera ahead of you so that you are always walking towards it – faces are more interesting than backs. And second, be standing fairly near the camera at the start, move towards it and walk out of shot past it. If you can edit, that gives you a choice of using it in two ways – cutting to it either as you turn and start to move or during your walk towards the camera. Both allow you to keep the shot short. Walking shots are useful but not if you have to hold them too long because there is no cutting point.

LEFT

4. Your next shot could be anything you fancy but it would be good to continue the movement. The skaters here are a feature of the square and give you an excuse for several quick shots of intriguing movement.

LEFT
5. To help change subject, use a closer shot of yourself or your partner. The close-up gives no clues in the frame of what should come next so you are free to cut to anything you like. One important point, however, because of the direction you are looking the following shot needs to be from overhead – the subjective point of view shot.

RIGHT
6. Luckily you have one – these children feeding the pigeons provide another typical sight in the square.

LEFT
7. And allow you several more pigeon shots.

LEFT
8. To end the sequence you might use the couple kissing or look around for some other occurrence, such as...

RIGHT
9...this man in the penguin costume talking to the real birds, demonstrating that a holiday in London has unpredictable moments!

AN ISLAND PORT

This sequence was shot on a Greek island which has comparatively few visitors – those who do visit it do so because they prefer smaller, less sophisticated resorts. Consequently, one of the enjoyable points about a holiday here is observing moments of local life. The sequence could only be planned in outline. One morning, some of the fishermen arrived to sell their catch; the activity generated gave a good opportunity to collect together many aspects of daily life in the tiny port.

The previous scene had been a group of friends playing beach games; luckily it had been noisy with a fair amount of movement so the slower port scene would make a good contrast. But the last shot had been tranquil – a girl settling back to read in the evening sun – so how do you make a good link?

RIGHT

1. Playing safe, the opening, of the boats approaching the jetty, was shot wide. In editing it was possible to make the link with sound – the noise of the boat's engine was faded up over the shot of the girl reading, continuing into the port shot.

RIGHT

2. The next cut was to this close shot of a fisherman calling out as the boat came near the jetty.

RIGHT

3. This quick shot of general activity taken after the boat had tied up was a cover shot to get to the next significant action ...

4 ... which was the weighing of the fish for sale. The intention was to keep rolling as the fish was wrapped, panning with it as ...

LEFT
5 ... it was handed to a customer. This took too much screen time and needed shortening. So the tape was rolled back to an edit point and a three-second close-up of a fish inserted; the camera was restarted as the fish was handed over. This ability to operate quickly cut out a boring 20 or 30 seconds.

RIGHT
6. Enough of the fish sale – time to move to something else! Quick cutaways of boats and other activities. To maintain both mood and sense of location the fish selling was dubbed as a low background to this shot, gradually fading under the succeeding pictures.

LEFT
7. From the cafe shot of people watching the port activity there was another sound change – a slow fade up of music.

RIGHT
8. The shot from inside the cafe is a bit of a teaser, bringing the music right up but delaying the cut to...

LEFT
9 ... the musician himself; the shots of him and those watching run for about 20 seconds.

10. The music continued over a cut to a shot of the other side of the harbour, an archaeological site. Using the music kept the transition smooth to this short sequence.

11. Tilting down closer shots of the columns ...

RIGHT

12 ... and exploring the site with longer shots. No zooms and only one pan! As the music came to its end ...

BELOW

13 ... cut to this neutral shot with the soft sound of the breeze. This is an image which allows any type of following sequence.

The sequence was edited in-camera, the only post-production work being on sound. Soundtracks were relaid and a sentence of commentary added. This was an enjoyable sequence to shoot. A number of positions and possible shots had been planned during strolls through the town over previous days, but being in the port with the camera when the fishermen arrived was pure luck. The foresight was to have the second reel of tape available to record sound. Two wildtracks were made after the picture shoot: two songs with the musician as well as the port soundtrack. The subsequent cuts to the musician were kept very short. This was because, as the music was to be relaid later, it would minimize any sync problems, especially of bow movements. Shooting the archaeological site the next day gave an opportunity to play the music overnight and get a feeling for the length and tempo of shots which would match it.

Section 8 The Family

The family obviously presents lots of potential for home video-making and allows you to capture all manner of activities and events as the years go by – for perpetuity.

CHILDREN

As the family grows up it is very natural to want a video record of them. Remember though, video is a different medium to the snapshot camera; it needs movement, so whatever the age of your children, do not pose them when you want to film them – instead show them in action.

Use your camcorder to observe, seizing the chance to take your shots when they are engrossed in an activity; alternatively arrange something for them to do which will take their attention away from the camera. This has the advantage of allowing you to shoot sequences more easily. Use wide angles to show the situation, medium shots to get a closer look at the activity and close-ups of their tasks or faces – all will flow naturally because you will have something to explain to your viewers. And while you are doing this, you will find that your children's personalities and characters will emerge.

Remember that your lens height should be the same as the subject's eyes; do not look down on children, get the camera on their level.

ABOVE and BELOW
Do not pose children; let your camera observe them involved in their own activities as they grow up.

PARTIES

It is the reason for the party that will decide how you should shoot it. Whether it is a child's birthday, a housewarming or a wedding anniversary, it will have a centrepiece which gives you a climax to work towards.

Make little sequences; show the arrival of the principal guests, have a scene of the children's games, show people in animated conversation. Try not to restrict yourself to two-shots; instead use the technique for shooting subjective shots (*see* section Telling a Story) of others in the conversation.

Do some Vox Pop interviews, asking two questions at the most – why they came and their views on the event celebrated by the party. For example, ask children what they enjoyed at the party. This is a device to change the pace of the material as well as allowing the guests to

talk to your audience.

Be ready when the important moment comes – the entry of the cake, the gifts or the speeches. Because it is the climax of the event, you need to plan your technical resources to ensure you do it justice. You may need to keep mobile for most of the shooting but to cover this important part ensure that you have enough light, that you have a mic positioned and a tripod for the camera.

Decide beforehand if you will record by day or artificial light (remember, pictures recorded in insufficient light will be noisy and copy badly). Increase room light with high wattage bulbs in existing fittings, supplementing them if necessary with more domestic lamps. If you use special video lights, bounce them from white ceilings (or even suitable walls) to keep a softer light and to preserve the party atmosphere.

If you edit afterwards, record an atmos wildtrack.

LEFT
Remember to have the lens at the children's eye height.

BELOW
Get party guests to talk to camera, but look for light-hearted interviews.

DAYS OUT

Holidays give you a relaxed opportunity to record happy events and show children at succeeding stages in their growth and development. So does the occasional day out. Use the camcorder to capture what you do and see – show the journey, your family and companions as they picnic, take fairground rides, go sightseeing – then end the video with the children's comments and assessments. You will find it fascinating for years to come!

ABOVE
Tell the story of your day out through the people you meet...

LEFT
...the forms of transport you take ...

RIGHT
...or what you see on the way.

Observing the natural world is an area ever-gaining in popularity. Whether television created or supported the interest, today's camcorders give everyone the chance to capture some aspect of this fascinating subject. City farms, nature trails, bird and wildlife sanctuaries, safari parks and your garden are all locations offering particular opportunities.

ZOOS AND NATURE RESERVES

Because the purpose of such a trip is observation, patience and stalking your prey are a part of the experience. Sanctuaries usually provide hides, but in locations where you are free to move around keep a low profile. Try to stay downwind of the animal so that it is less aware of you and assess its habits to predict its movements.

Aim to show something of the animal's habitat then take close-ups of its activities. Feeding times make good pictures – watering places will give shots as the animals gather. For animals in public parks, take meat or breadcrumbs as bait. After feeding and in hot weather many creatures will snooze which gives opportunities for other types of shot.

Use a tripod or monopod in static positions and the image stabilizer if you have to move around. Use fast shutter if you want to analyze movements; macro focus will be necessary for small creatures. For shooting animals behind protective barriers, avoid the AF (autofocus) focusing on the bars, netting or glass by using manual controls (or consult the camcorder instructions). Remember to check on any restrictions or regulations in wildlife reserves such as not opening car windows to take shots in safari parks; many will be for the benefit of the animals, others are for your safety.

Do not open car windows to take shots in safari parks. However charming they look, animals can be very unpredictable.

PETS

Shoot pets in action, stalking them or getting help to create a situation for them to play. And remember to lower the camcorder to the pet's eyeline.

ABOVE
Keep the lens at the animal's eye level – if you can!

BELOW
Do not always go for close-ups; showing something of the habitat also provides interest.

Section 10 Sport and Outdoor Events

Sports and outdoor events (processions, festivals, carnivals) are all about movement and are natural video subjects. Their challenge is that you only have one chance to record them and things can happen fast! You may be prevented from using your camcorder at big events but local ones can offer more opportunities and cooperation.

BEFORE THE EVENT
- Find out what will happen – when and where.
- Select your positions – they determine your shots and coverage.
- Make proper arrangements – particularly ensure that you can be where you want to be at the appropriate time.

SELECTING POSITIONS
High positions will:
- Reveal the patterns of movement – useful for games on courts and pitches.
- Show the layout – for track and circuit sports and also processions.

Low positions will:
- Isolate individuals and dramatize actions.

Bends and curves:
- Give you a choice of shot, from the front as things approach and from the side as they pass (check lefts and rights).

Court and pitch lines:
- Sidelines give the best all-purpose angles – shoot from one side only to avoid crossing the line. If you have only one position it must be the centre, then turn around for spectator shots looking left and right.

- End lines are good for attacking play, goal shots and tennis serves – for cricket and baseball be above head level to see bowlers and pitchers.

Finishes:
- The further from the finish the more likely it is that people will get in the way. To avoid obstruction, get close (ensure your shot is wide enough) or high.

Check, that the chosen position:
- Does not confuse the viewer's sense of direction. Ensure that for pitch and court games you do not cross the line or for other events that your lefts and rights are correct, maintaining the participants direction of movement (*see* section Telling a Story).
- Gives you good light; remember to avoid confusing shadows or the sun shining into your lens.

CAMERAWORK
Remember that your coverage is intended to observe and explain the action. Start with wide angle shots to set the action then use narrative shots which contain the scene. Move in to closer shots to catch the excitement of the event but generally avoid close-ups and shots of individuals unless the viewer would be confused without them.

Remember the rule: do not change shot unless the reason for change is visible. When covering events this usually means cutting to another viewpoint because the action has passed the camera position, panning to follow movement or zooming in or out to contain it. Beware of zooming too often however; in sports coverage, zoom only in time with the players, starting and stopping your movement with theirs.

Avoid repeating camera movements without reason. If during a procession you started every shot with the vehicle approaching and panned with it past your camera position it would be boring. Instead, vary it with different angles and shot lengths from the same position and use cutaways to change the rhythm. Keep shots steady, using a tripod or monopod, or for hand-held shots the image stabilizer. And use fast shutter speeds to analyze movements if the video is to be used for training.

The movement of sport makes it a natural for video.

Positions determine what you can shoot at any time.

This high position shows the field.

A position on the bend is good for track events.

A low position – isolates individual athletes

Touch line position – good for football.

Finishes – get close and above head level, if possible

A wide angle with plenty of atmosphere to start this student rag event.

Get close but beware individual close-ups on continuous action.

Follow the action until it is best to let it go out of shot, giving you a cutting point to the next moment.

Do not be tempted to zoom in on a shot like this – there is no single point of interest.

If you shoot many of the groups passing this same camera position you could have the problem of repeating camera movements.

One answer is to frame the shot in other ways.

TELL A STORY

Give shape and drama to your coverage with additional material. For example, build the tension before the event, taking shots of people preparing and arriving as well as of the course or ground. Use commentary to identify places and people, interviewing participants or spectators. Ask what they anticipate and consider to be the significance of the event for themselves and others?

If editing in-camera:
- Shoot cutaways of spectator reaction at the start or end of sequences to bridge time gaps or changes of location.
- Use an audio recorder to record crowd and location noises; use these to smooth over picture changes.

If editing after shooting:
- Shoot plenty of cutaways to cover edits.
- Record crowd and atmos wildtrack in each location to smooth sound edits and to back commentary.

COMMENTARY

Record this during the event to capture excitement and presence or after to ensure information is correct. Use an external mic suitable for close work.

The crowds assembling for the Tunisian Independence Day celebrations in Midoun. These shots can build the tension to the main events.

Use commentary over early scenes to identify places and people.

Shoot plenty of cutaway details.

Ensure that you record lots of atmos sound.

Record commentary on the spot to capture more atmosphere.

"Can you record it for us?" This is a frequent request to camcorder owners from friends and acquaintances who want to see what their play or exhibition or indoor demonstration looked like. It can be fun to do but there is more to it than placing the camcorder in front of them and letting it run.

CAMERA POSITIONS

- At the front and centre, essential for dance.
- Lens height at eye level (difficult in some auditoriums).

Where seeing the eyes of performers is important choose between slightly higher or lower angles. For dance, being above shows the choreographic patterns: too high foreshortens the figure spoiling the line of the body.

LIGHT

Ensure there is enough. Remember, if there is too little light your picture will be noisy and copy badly, focus will be shallow and difficult to maintain. Lectures and demonstrations are often underlit or poorly lit; when arranging the shoot ask for enough light for your camera. Theatre performances may also present problems because of their contrasty and coloured lighting. If you are making a special recording, ask if the electrician will reduce contrasts and slightly overlight.

CAMERAWORK

- Use a tripod.
- Start with a wide shot of the stage or main area. As the performers move or enter, match the speed of their moves to zoom in to a long or medium shot. Avoid making zoom changes noticeable. Use further moves (walking, gestures, turns) to zoom in or out. Never pan or zoom unless the subject is moving, time your movement exactly with theirs. Stay as close as you dare to the main area of action. Unless there is one performer onstage for a long time, avoid single shots or close-ups. As long as you have the essential action framed, do not be afraid to let people walk in and out of the shot.

Especially during lectures, if objects or slides are used for illustration:

1. If you cannot edit, slowly zoom in on them and zoom out for the next part of the talk.
2. If you can edit, record the performance/lecture simultaneously on an audio recorder (feed the sound from camcorder to audio recorder or vice-versa, depending on which gives the best result). Change shot to and away from the illustration very rapidly – or arrange with the speaker to shoot the illustrations before or after. Record additional cutaway audience shots (during the introduction to the speaker or other suitable time). Use insert edit to put in the audience cutaways and/or illustrations with the accompanying sound from the audio recorder.

SOUND

Use a separate mic (or mics) rather than the camcorder's built-in one.

For stage performances, hang a mic above the stage and in front of the proscenium; alternatively use a stand to put it at the front of the stage (place it so that it cannot be knocked by costumes or stage moves. Avoid putting it on the stage or it may pick up the noise of footsteps). Omni-directional and two-sided mics in these positions should pick up both voices and audience reaction. For dance performances, if possible get an additional sound feed direct from the music source.

For theatre in the round and performances which have the audience on two or three sides, you will need to put up a mic to cover each area the performers face.

For lecturers and demonstrators attach a personal mic (radio if possible).

TOP THREE
Contrasty theatre lighting often gives pictures lacking in detail or overexposed highlights.

RIGHT
High angles show the patterns of dance routines.

Section 12 **Drama**

Making a dramatic video is the nearest thing to making a feature film and carries overtones of glamour and prestige. Some amateur video groups specialize in making dramas and do very well at it. Ideally, you need a good team of interested people plus high-end domestic or semi-professional equipment, especially for editing. If that is a future aim, you can get some creative enjoyment now by creating a simple drama or comedy with the family or friends.

Start small is the best advice. Go for for ideas which can be told in less than five minutes with only two or three characters. Set it in your house, garden or an accessible location. Write a script, but avoid inhibiting your creativity at the start by attempting to write shots or technical jargon. Write the dialogue (if any) down the left hand side of the page, the visuals and movements on the other; this will make it easy to analyze it into separate shots. Keep it simple; write: 'We see ...' and 'We hear ...' Think visual, revealing character and plot in actions.

When you have a script you like, work out a method of shooting. Choose a location and decide the actors' moves, then plot the main shots, identifying the narrative and subjective ones. Think where you will position the camera to get your shots. If you edit in-camera chose a bold narrative style which does not need much cutting back and forth to characters on separate lines of dialogue, or quick, subtle reaction shots.

With the information assembled, list your technical requirements.

List who is helping and what they will do; you will need a director, a camera operator, a sound operator to handle the mic, a lighting person (if only to hold a reflector) and at least one extra person (to do what others have forgotten, to cover extra jobs, to make tea and to keep everyone relaxed!)

Decide if you have the equipment you need, or if you need to change the script to work within your capability.

Ensure you can get the camera, mic and other equipment in the positions you need them.

List the furniture and set dressings, props and costumes you need – as well as the way to borrow or acquire them.

Calculate the time you need to

Finchley Cine Video Society at work on a WWII drama.

Shoot simple stories with easy to find locations.

On the recording day ensure everyone knows what to do.

Mark each take; any simple method will do, this is a child's slate marked with chalk.

complete the shooting.

However rough and ready it is, give everyone involved a script; they can then work out what they need to do and suggest improvements.

On the day:
Work to a plan and a timetable.
Follow the professional routine of director's calls, then everyone knows where they are.
Call:
- Standby (to mean that you will either rehearse or record within 30 or 40 seconds).
- Relax Everyone (if there is a hitch).
- Rehearsal (if that is what it is).
- This is a Take or Recording (to ensure everyone knows).
- Turnover or Run Camera (to start).
- Running (from the Recordist to confirm).
- Action (for the performers to start).
- Cut (to stop only when you are sure you have the shot, plus five seconds for safety).

If you edit post-production, mark shots at their beginning. Avoid taking individual short shots; instead shoot long sections without stopping. Shoot narrative sections entire, doing the cutaways or reaction shots after. If the scene comprises sub-jective shots, shoot the whole from one side then repeat the whole section from the complementary angle (called the reverse angle); it will save shooting time and give greater choice for editing.

Keep track of what you have shot by marking the director's script. Finish within the planned time; it encourages people to come again!

Section 13 Making a Music Video

You will make a better quality pop music video if you can edit efficiently. The skills to concentrate on are sound recording, imaginative camerawork and creative editing.

Start with shots of the group – playing to an audience – in a studio or out on location. Then interpret the number they are playing through situations which make a sequence or images; when juxtaposed in editing, these should amplify the ideas.

Set a style for the number then try to keep to it throughout in the settings, the performers' clothes, the camerawork and the image processing and editing.

If out on locations, look for a setting with atmosphere which frees the group to perform. Research these carefully to ensure that you can use the technical facilities you want on the site and also get permission to video.

Get as much technical help as you can to create memorable images. Use camera movement to create differing moods or excitement and use graphics, animation or post-production editing processes. To give a unity to pictures shot at differing times and places, use video processors to change colours or posterize images. Cut the images in time with, or creating a counterpoint to, the music.

Shoot the video with the musicians (and other performers) performing to an audio playback of the number; this can be done for short as well as long takes, giving you pictures with sync sound to edit (this will require accurate editing). Or shoot non-sync pictures and edit them to timings taken from the music.

Finally, dub the music.

Explore unusual images with wide angle lenses. For other visual effects use filters coloured light or change the light balance.

LEFT
Use atmospheric locations.

FAR LEFT
Multiple images can be produced with filters.

Section 14 **News**

Camcorder users are increasingly finding themselves at news-making incidents; some have found themselves to be the only people with a camera as a drama erupts, others attending public events covered by press and TV have found themselves to be close to the unexpected with a view which could not be anticipated by the professionals.

Television news companies frequently use camcorder material to support and supplement professional footage; if you are faced with an incident which may be newsworthy what do you do?

1. Start recording; check focus.
2. Switch off your data display and check main camera settings.
3. Keep covering the action, avoid unnecessary zooming and use standard camera moves. Do not stop to reframe shots when things are still happening. If you must, make big changes decisively and quickly (*see* also section Sport and Outdoor Events).
4. Avoid actions which hamper the work of police and emergency services.
5. Remember your own safety. Cameras do not offer protection from violence; indeed they sometimes attract it. Quick thinking gets more pictures than bravura or bravery.
6. Be sensitive to victims and others involved in incidents.

ABOVE and BELOW
However dramatic the event remember basic technicalities eg. In the top picture. If you zoom in on the people use backlight compensation.

7. Avoid being unpleasant to other camera users – you have no special rights.
8. Never recreate incidents.
9. Within 15 to 30 minutes of the start of an incident, use a nearby phone to contact a TV newsroom (get a companion to do this if possible). Avoid leaving the scene yourself until events are over. State factually and without hype what coverage you have. If they are interested, ask how you should proceed.
10. If payment is important, discuss this after the material has been seen and accepted – but before it has been shown!
11. Do not go looking for news, unless you turn professional.

Whether you edit in-camera or have the ability to assemble your video afterwards by editing, this section shows you ways to do it. It also gives advice on how to put that extra polish on the show with music commentary and titles.

Video editing can be of two sorts:

NON LINEAR

These systems use computers – the material to be edited is transferred from the original videos to the computer where it can be edited in a cut and paste way. If you wish to delete or insert material after you have put a scene together there is no difficulty – the computer closes the gaps. The computer programme will also cope with a full range of mixes and wipes eliminating the need for a third video machine; the finished result is then copied on to the master tape. The limitation of the system is that, at the time of writing, it uses so much computing power that it can only edit short sections at one time. An affordable non-linear system has not yet been developed for the domestic market.

LINEAR

This is the transfer from an original tape to a Master Edit tape of the sections of picture and sound which you need for the final programme, using a player machine and a recorder. With this method you start at the beginning of your story and continue to the end. The limitations of this system are:
- If you make a mistake you may need to re-edit everything from that point.
- To edit using more than cuts or fades (eg, mixes) you need three machines, two players and one recorder.

Linear editing uses two different technical systems related to the control track.

Assemble editing: this means recording your pictures on the edit tape in the order of the final programme. The control track is laid at the same time and the stability of the edits is maintained by each new picture electronically sticking itself to the control track of the preceding one. Because the control track is not continuous, spaces cannot be left for the insertion of material at a later stage, nor

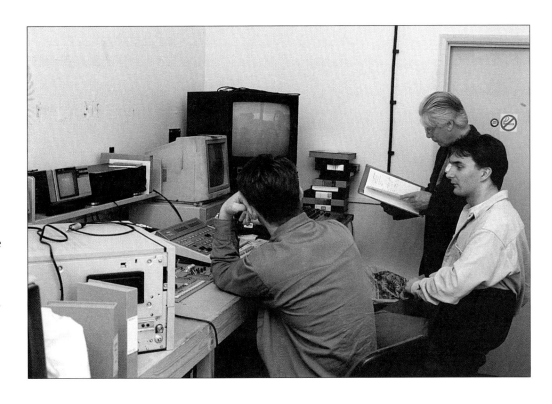

can additional or replacement pictures be dropped in later.

Insert editing: to use this system you must record onto a tape which has been 'blacked', meaning a continuous control track has been recorded. As you edit the pictures are held stable by electronically attaching themselves onto the unbroken control track. This means that you can record pictures anywhere along its length, leaving gaps to be filled later. More practically it means that cutaways and other shots can be dropped in – inserted – at any stage in editing.

EQUIPMENT

Effective editing means having equipment which will allow you to make picture changes accurately, preferably on the exact frame you have chosen. Domestic video equipment does not always offer that accuracy. Simple systems may be accurate only to +/- 12 to 25 frames (half to one second). Systems using timecode should offer an accuracy of +/- two to five frames, depending on the model and its maintenance.

This is an indication of what sorts of editing you could do and the type of equipment you would need to achieve it.

If you have edited in-camera (and your camcorder has the facilities) you will need:
- A monitor screen (your TV set).
- An audio recorder/player.

This should enable you to:
- Add titles from the camera memory.
- Dub a new or extra soundtrack to add music, commentary, background sounds and post-sync dialogue (see Sound Editing).

For basic editing after shooting you will need:
- A recording VCR.
- A playback VCR (this can be your camcorder).
- A monitor screen for each (it is possible to use your TV set and the camcorder viewfinder).
- An audio recorder/player. (*Adding a sound mixer will allow you more flexibility and sophistication*).

This will enable you to:
- Transfer material from one machine to another and assemble it in a different order.
- Insert edit titles and cutaways.
- Dub a new or extra soundtrack to add music, commentary, post-sync dialogue and background sounds. BUT without using timecode it is unlikely that this set-up would permit any finely timed edits.

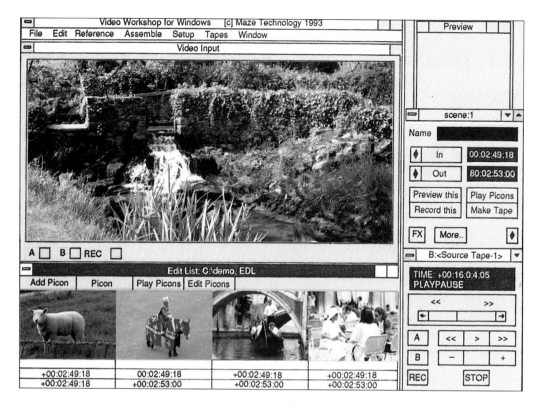

The fast developing computer market offers a widening range of programmes for video makers. This typical menu screen for an editing programme shows current and stored shots with their timings.

For good control of post-production editing (ie. +/- two to five frames accuracy): you would need:

- A hi-band recorder VCR with edit control, insert edit, audio dub and time-code facilities plus a real-time counter.
- A hi-band player VCR with time-code and TBC facilities plus a real-time counter (better still, use the same make and model as the recorder VCR).
- A monitor screen for each.
- An edit controller or a computer with an edit control programme (unless your VCR has a built-in controller). The edit controller controls both play and record VCRs, first separately, to let you select precise frames as cutting points and enter them into the memory, and then synchronized so that their motors run back or forward to the memorized points, lock together and give an exact run-up and edit. It will also have the facility to rehearse the edit without recording it.
- A vision mixer, to enable you to do a range of picture changes like fades and wipes (but to do mixes you may need another VCR player).
- A titling outfit or a computer with suitable graphics and animation packages.
- A genlock (for use with the PC, allowing its output to be controlled and used without picture

disturbance).
- An audio recorder/player (analogue open reel machines offer greatest flexibility or multi-channel cassette decks).
- Audio playback machines for CDs, cassettes and discs.
- An audio mixer (possibly with some equalization facility).

NB – It is possible to replace all these items by one PC with a full non-linear edit programme.

COMPUTER PROGRAMMES
The PC market is fast developing both hard and software for the domestic video user. Currently available programmes include:
- Formats for scriptwriting.
- Titlers.
- Animations.
- Sound effects editing.
- Music composing.
- Combined image and sound mixer/enhancer/effects generators.
- Edit controllers with memory (you load your edit list – it will edit your programme).

METHODS AND TECHNIQUES
Use Commentary
A spoken commentary can give information which cannot be shown in picture or which is missing from the interviews or other recorded content. It

can also add colour with an element of personality or wholeheartedly personalize the programme. But remember, video is a medium of moving images; it is these that must give the important information. A commentary can only supplement the visuals.

When writing or speaking commentary choose the points you want to make and the moments you make them with care and economy, using simple, easy-to-understand language and restricting yourself to factual information. Opinions can only be reported and summarized with extreme brevity in commentary – they come over best in interviews. Also avoid dissertations and the explanation of arguments – this should be done by a person in vision, or by visual demonstration.

USE MUSIC.
Music can add pace and colour to your video programme altering mood and suggesting emotion. It can smooth transitions or jolt tranquillity. Grand music can reinforce the pomp of a ceremony while light-hearted music tends to undermine its pomposity. Use it with a consistent style but only when its power is appropriate. Nothing is worse than the programme with continuous background music, sounding as if a radio has been left on! *Beware – the use of music, lyrics and arrangements by composers now alive, or who have died within the last 50 years, is covered by the copyright laws. So too are most performances of any recorded music, lyrics and arrangements. Basically, if you show your tape in public you should clear copyright, usually by paying a fee – seek advice from the publisher of the recording or music. Amateur video makers belonging to a club or society may find that their group has special and inexpensive arrangements to cover this. There are also recordings on sale of copyright free music (and sound effects). They are often advertized in amateur video magazines.*

TITLES AND OTHER GRAPHICS.
Titles add a professional touch to video making. Apart from giving names at the beginning and end of your production they can be used within it to clarify sections or give explanations with tables, diagrams and maps.

A blackboard with a set of white letters which can be attached to it is all that is needed for quite sophisticated

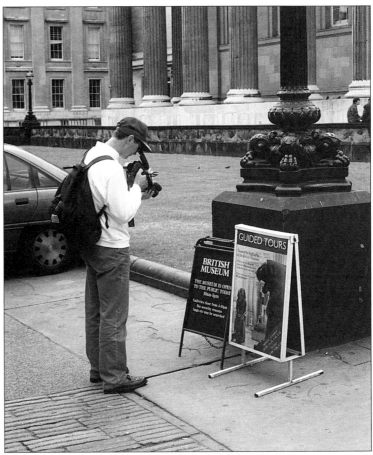

When shooting remember the sign boards and street signs on location – these give ready-made and appropriate titles.

titling effects. Positioning and size can be controlled by framing, letters can be animated and colours can be generated either in recording or editing. Greater variety can be introduced by inlaying the letters in to your pictures. Shoot special background pictures for titles by deliberately softening the focus to let the lettering stand out more.

For those who want to use many different typefaces, as well as drop shadows, titles which scroll up, down or across the frame and animations, there are many PC programmes to choose from, as well as some video effects machines with titling ability.

EDITING CONVENTIONS

Whether you edit in-camera or after shooting the following points apply:

- Aim to keep each shot on the screen only for as long as it is interesting – an average time is eight seconds, but sometimes only two or three seconds. (The eye can explore the picture very quickly, consequently having seen a shot it expects some change – a movement of the person or the camera; should that not happen look for a reason to make a cut to another shot. It could be a different length or angle of the same person, or a shot of other people – or objects – involved in the action.)
- There must always be a reason or a motivation for a picture change. To decide the exact moment or the type of change appropriate, be guided by the following rules.

Make the cut on:
- A move.
- A look.
- A sound (eg, a word of dialogue or a musical beat).

The cut on a move
Example A
If a person within the shot rises and moves out of frame we want to know where they have gone, so cut on the movement to a wider shot to show their new position.

Example B
If someone gestures to something outside the frame we want to know who or what it is, so cut on the move either to a wider shot to include that person or object, or to a separate shot of them.

The cut on a look
Example A
A person within shot is speaking but suddenly looks off camera. The audience want to know the reason so cut on the look to see (as a separate shot or a wider one to include) what caused them to look.

Example B
Two characters are walking along a road, one falls and then looks at the other; cut on the look to the other person to discover their reaction.

The cut on a sound
Example A
A person in shot asks a question of another – cut to the other person to see their answer or reaction.

Example B
In a music sequence whether the change comes after a number of bars or on an instrumental entry, the cut normally comes on the beat.

Avoid:
- Cutting between shots during camera movements (especially pans, tilts and zooms).
- Cutting between a shot during a camera move to a static shot.
- Jump cuts – that is, incomplete body movements or movements started in one shot but not seen in the following shot.

Make a mix (dissolve):
- To indicate a lapse in time.
- When getting from one scene to another when there could have been a time lapse.
- Going to or from title captions.

Fade in and out:
- To indicate a longer time lapse than a mix.

Big show or home video – the same editing rules apply.

SOUND
When fading in or out on a scene the sound should also fade in or out at the same time; occasionally sound can fractionally precede vision at the start of a scene.

EDITING IN-CAMERA AND AFTER SHOOTING
If you have edited in-camera there are several ways to improve or add sophistication to your programme without the acquisition of too much extra equipment.

Insert Editing
You will need two machines, then, provided your camera or your home VCR has the insert edit facility, you can add pictures and sound into your already recorded material. Long takes can have cutaways added, missing or better material can be dropped in, pictures and sound could be edited separately.

The technique of laying picture and sound separately depends on the type of VCR you are using for editing. Most VCR machines with insert edit facility record over the existing picture and all soundtracks. A few will leave one of the tracks, in which case you could first record the desired section of soundtrack (itself edited if necessary) using the audio dub facility. Then insert a selection of appropriate pictures. Where the insert edit erases all soundtracks you need to time the track, then lay down the pictures for that duration first. The soundtrack is laid last.

Sound Editing
By paying attention to sound even the most basic assemblage of shots can be given point by commentary; a smoothness of picture change by relaying atmos and more colour by the addition of music.

Even if your camcorder has only one sound recording track, as long as it has the audio dub facility, it is possible to re-record a new more complex soundtrack. If you have atmos or sound effects you wish to keep, transfer sections of the existing track to an audio recorder. It is then possible, using the recorder and other sound sources, to play back through a mixer a soundtrack of commentary, effects, music and atmos. Use the dub facility to replace the original soundtrack without disturbing the picture. With practice using this system, it is even possible to get a performer to post-sync dialogue or songs (re-recorded with the new sound matching lip movements).

Beware - most equipment will not have the accuracy to transfer an original dialogue track and re-record it, nor any atmos track which has points which must synchronize exactly.

For clarity and to avoid tiring the ears of your audience, keep music and atmos tracks well below the level of dialogue and commentary.

If you were unable to fade picture from/to black at the beginning or end of a scene you can achieve a similar effect by replacing a section of the sound at that point. Fade it in from, or to, silence where the picture fade would have come.

If you have both hi-fi and linear (ordinary mono) soundtrack facilities on your machine, then you have the possibility of using three sound channels separately and can achieve sophisticated results.

Leave dialogue, or sounds which must synchronize, on the track which will not be erased when using the audio dub facility. Then use audio dub to add sounds to the existing track. If the replaceable track is mono use a mixer to blend additional sounds; if it is stereo you can maintain better control if you put the most important sound (eg, commentary) on one channel and the rest (music/atmos/effects) on the other. If necessary, balances between the channels can then be adjusted on playback and when copying.

EDITING AFTER SHOOTING

Plan your edit before you start. Having a clear idea of your shots and sequences beforehand enables you to keep control of the pace and therefore the audience's interest in your production.

Review copies of the original tapes to annotate your script or compile an edit list. This logging process should enable you to note:
- The start and finish of each shot to be

Use specially recorded sound and atmospheres to mix with commentary or dialogue.

used and where to find it on the original tapes.
- Details of the sounds to be added to the original track, each section of commentary, every sound effect, all wildtracks of atmos or speech, where each should start and finish and what they are played in from (eg., video, CD, audio cassette or disc).

Edit in sequence; do not be tempted to leave gaps for material to come. If you do not have the shots, it is better to postpone the edit until you do.

Replay edited sections at regular intervals. Assess the pace, spot mistakes and remedy problems whilst they are only minor.

Section 16 Foreign Affairs – Going Abroad and Exchanging Tapes

Taking your video camera and equipment abroad means that you must check two things carefully:

- That the equipment that you wish to use will operate on the electricity supply of the places you wish to visit. Even if you operate on batteries you will probably have to recharge them.
- Different countries use different technical video colour standards. The three major ones are PAL, SECAM and NTSC (see below]) This means, for example, that if you intend to visit the USA you would not be able to connect your UK (PAL) camcorder to a local (NTSC) television set, or vice versa. Unless you have a colour viewfinder or can find a dual standard machine where you are going, checking your tapes for colour in another country may mean taking a

PAL portable monitor along with you. Differing national technical standards also mean that you cannot play back tapes from other systems unless you have a dual standard VTR (such domestic machines are not widely used in the UK). If you wish to exchange your own cassettes with family or friends overseas you will need to check the standard they operate on (see the table below). If it is different the tape will need to be converted and a copy made in the new standard – this should be done professionally. Find a duplicating or facilities house in video magazine advertisements or a classified telephone directory.

NB – Although there are two different PAL systems, all PAL tapes should be

compatible. SECAM tapes will play back on PAL machines (and vice versa) but only in black and white. All other systems are incompatible.

Sometimes overseas video equipment prices can appear to be very attractive but to assess them properly you will need to know:

- Its operating standard (PAL, NTSC or SECAM?) and whether it is compatible with your home standard.
- Whether its electricity standard is compatible with yours. Is it 50 or 60 phase and what is the operating voltage?
- How much Customs tax and VAT will you be charged when you come home.
- Whether it has any guarantee and if so who will honour it back home.

WORLD COUNTRIES LISTED BY THEIR TELEVISION SYSTEMS

PAL

Abu Dhabi	Afghanistan
Algeria	Argentina
Austria	Australia
Bahrain	Bangladesh
Belgium	Brazil (PAL M)
Brunei	Canary Islands
China	Cyprus
Denmark	Eire (PAL 1)
Finland	Germany (also SECAM)
Ghana	Gibraltar
Greece	Hong Kong (PAL 1)
Iceland	India
Israel	Italy
Indonesia	Jordan
Kenya	Kuwait
Liberia	Madeira
Malaysia	Malawi
Malta	Mozambique (PAL 1)
Netherlands	Nigeria
New Zealand	Norway
Pakistan	Paraguay
Portugal	Qatar
Sierra Leone	Singapore

Spain	Sri Lanka
South Africa (PAL 1)	
Sudan	Sweden
Switzerland	Tanzania (PAL1)
Thailand	Tibet
Turkey	Uganda
UAE	UK (PAL 1)
Uraguay	Yemen
States of former Yugoslavia	
Zambia	Zimbabwe

SECAM

Bulgaria	
Commonwealth of Independent States (and states of former USSR)	
Czech Republic	Egypt
France	Germany (also PAL)
Hungary	Iran
Iraq	Laos
Lebanon	Luxembourg
Monaco	Mongolia
Morocco	Poland
Romania	Saudi Arabia
Slovakia	Tunisia
Zaire	

NTSC

Alaska	Bahamas
Barbados	Bermuda
Burma	Canada
Chile	Colombia
Costa Rica	Cuba
Dominican Rep.	Ecuador
El Salvador	Greenland
Guatemala	Haiti
Hawaii	Honduras
Jamaica	Japan
Korea (South)	Mexico
Nicaragua	Panama
Peru	Philippines
Puerto Rico	Surinam
Taiwan	USA
Venezuela	

Against the Light To shoot with the light behind the scene or subject. At its most extreme it results in a silhouette.

AGC See Automatic Gain Control.

Ambient Sound Naturally occurring sound.

Angle of Acceptance The width of the angle of view of a lens measured horizontally.

Antenna (US) Aerial (UK).

Anti-Flare Spray used to prevent mirrors, glass or bright surfaces from reflecting light back into the camera.

Aspect Ratio Ratio of the width of the picture compared to its height. The current TV ratio is 4 x 3; the coming HDTV widescreen ratio is 16 x 9.

Assemble Edit Creation of a video sequence by recording shots one after the other (see RAE).

Atmos (Atmosphere) Sound term – the background or ambient sound of a scene.

Attenuator Device for reducing an electronic signal without distortion.

Autocue Trade name of prompter.

Automatic Gain Control A sound system which automatically increases the volume control for soft sounds and turns it down to prevent the loudest from distorting. Its effect can be very unnatural as it cannot distinguish relative importance, thus it may 'turn up' unwanted background noises but 'turn down' shouted words of dialogue. (Not to be confused with a Limiter.)

Back Focus The adjustment of (usually) a zoom lens to ensure that its image is correctly focused on the image plane throughout the whole of its range.

Barn Doors Hinged flaps which can be placed or attached in front of a lamp to enable its light to be controlled.

Bars The coloured vertical stripes of saturated colour used by engineers to adjust or align vision equipment for matched performance.

Bg (Background) Actions, settings or sounds behind the principal or foreground activity.

Betacam Professional video recorder developed by Sony.

Black (verb) See Black and Burst below.

Black and Burst. A video signal with the required synchronizing information for a colour picture but where the picture is black. Tapes prepared for insert editing must be 'blacked' by recording this signal continuously for the length of intended recording.

Boom Microphone support mounting – an upright column supporting a sophisticated telescopic mic arm mounted on a wheeled frame with an adjustable height platform for the boom operator. (See also Fish-pole and Lazy Arm.)

Bus Engineering term for a complete audio or video channel

Character Generator A device for making letters or signs on the screen electronically.

Chromakey A trade name which now describes a process. Colour separation overlay is the means by which areas of different cameras or image sources can be combined into a single picture. Usually a specific shade of a single colour in the first picture is used as a trigger. When the scanning line reaches that colour in the first picture it refuses to accept information from source one but puts in the picture information from source two. (Not to be confused with a Superimposition.)

Contrast Ratio The number of distinguishable tonal steps between lightest and darkest that the video picture can register.

Control Track A continuous signal recorded on the video tape to ensure it runs accurately to speed.

Fish Pole Hand-held telescopic microphone pole used for following moving sound sources. Most often seen on location shooting. (See also Boom and Lazy Arm.)

Flags Flat boards, often cut into shapes, used to cause shadows from lamps. Unlike Barn Doors they are used slightly further away from the lamp to throw more defined shadows.

Fluid Head A tripod head where the movement is damped by a lubricant oil. The cheaper 'fluid effect' heads imitate the process by the use of low-friction coated bearings.

Flying Erase Heads An extra VCR or camcorder recording head used to produce clean picture cuts in editing.

Genlock A device allowing signals from different pieces of equipment to be used in combination without picture disturbance. Used to lock different cameras together for simultaneous recording and also as a computer accessory to superimpose graphics over video images.

HDTV High Definition Television. Picture system offering a clearer image by using more scanning lines. The main competing systems use a 16 x 9 aspect ratio and 1250 lines/50 fields (Europe), 1125 lines/60 fields (Japan) and 1050 lines/60 fields (USA).

Headroom (1) The space in the framing of a camera shot above the subject's head.

Headroom (2) A limit set for an electronic signal, usually allowing a safety margin above any measured or anticipated peak.

High (or Hi-) Band Video recording format using an increased signal band width (and improved

Horizontal Resolution   A way of expressing picture clarity based on the fineness of the horizontal lines capable of being seen, recorded or transmitted by a piece of equipment. Low-band video systems reproduce about 240-260 lines, high band about 400 lines. Broadcast quality systems should reproduce a minimum of 700 lines.

Jog/Shuttle   Control (usually like a large dial) on edit controllers or edit-VCRs used for selecting precise frames in the editing process.

Lazy Arm   Fish Pole used in a simple supporting upright. Most often used on location shooting as an alternative to a Boom.

Limiter   Device for preventing either sound or vision signals going above a pre-determined ceiling. (Not to be confused with AGC).

Low (or Lo-) Band   See High Band.

Monitor (noun)   A TV screen without the capacity to receive off-air.

Monitor (verb)   To watch or listen carefully to programme material.

Noise   Random unwanted signals, generated within equipment or resulting from external interference, which is seen as oscillating grain in the picture or heard as hiss in sound.

NTSC   National Television System Committee – the US standard, 525-line YV system. Sometimes ironically described as Never Twice the Same Colour!

OOV   Out of Vision – used to describe something out of the camera picture.

PAL   Phase Alternate Line – a development of the (US) NTSC TV system. (See NTSC and SECAM.)

PCM   Pulse Code Modulation – additional sound recording system available on some VCRs and Hi8 camcorders.

Post-production   All work done on a production after the main recording (or shoot). Usually creation of graphics and titling, post synchronization of dialogue, creation and recording of music and sound effects, any reshooting and final picture and sound editing – plus publicity, paperwork and the accounts!

Prompter   A device for displaying a performer's script over or near the camera lens so that it can be read as if memorized. Simple systems use a paper scroll, turned by hand or motorized. Others use computer generated text displayed on a monitor screen.

RAE   Random Assemble Edit – a system in-built in some camcorders and VCRs which is capable of storing edit points and then controlling both source and destination video machines in the assemble edit process.

RCTC   Rewritable Consumer Time Code (pronounced arc-tic). This is Sony's timecode system; it can be rewritten after shooting.

Rule of Thirds   A guide for composition which suggests that if the frame is divided into nine areas, by imagining three equally spaced horizontal and three vertical lines, the points of most visual interest will lie where the lines cross.

SECAM   Sequential Couleur a Memoire – 625-line TV system developed in France (see also PAL and NTSC).

Set (verb)   To build or otherwise prepare the setting(s) and cameras ready for a rehearsal or recording.

Set (noun)   Scenery or performing area.

Soft (1)   Unfocused, scattered light.

Soft (2)   Slightly out of focus.

SMPTE   A timecode system used professionally.

Super (Superimposition)   The combination of the whole frame output from two cameras or image sources.

TBC   Time Base Corrector – a device which can correct unstable or unsynchronized video signals. Some VCRs have them built in, making them the best machines for playing in to an editing system.

Timecode   A system for writing invisible identification codes to each video frame. A timecode-compatible edit recorder enables frame-accurate editing. The most usual domestic versions are RCTC and VITC (SMPTE is a professional, version).

VITC   Vertical Interval Timecode – timecode used by Panasonic and other manufacturers. Can only be written at the time of shooting (unlike RCTC).

VCR   Domestic video (cassette) recorder.

Wildtrack   A non-synchronized soundtrack. A typical use is to record ambient sound from a particular location to give an authentic sound to a sequence shot in a studio, or to even out the background sound from several shots taken at different times when the location background sound varied.

Camcorder Symbols and their Meaning

Symbol	Meaning
▷	Playback
▷▷	Fast forward/ cue, search forward
◁◁	Rewind/ review, search back
△	Eject
▷	Slow frames
‖	Pause
■	Stop
○	Record
○‖	Record/pause
●●●●"	Index mark
●●●●	Index search
●●●●●	Index scan
✳	Index erase

Symbol	Meaning
— ⋅ ✕ — ⋅ —	Tracking adjust
— ▷ — —	Auto tracking
⏻	Standby (off)
⏼	On
⏚	Timer
○	Go to zero
— | — | — |	Count display reset
⊠	Audio mute
◢	Volume +or –
→ ⏻	Auto off
◑	Contrast
☀	Brightness
⊛	Colour
⌢	Headphone output

Symbol	Meaning
⌢+	Headphone volume
— — ⁄ —	Manual control by menu
[→|←]	Return to standard settings
[N]	Return to standard settings
[+]	Channel display on
[....]	Mode display on
V∧	Channel select
[←]	AV (line in)
[....]	Audio Dub

ACKNOWLEDGEMENTS

All Action Pictures
Pages 10 below, 61left, 62 middle,top right, bottom right.

Nadia Hilton
Pages 42-45, 58 both, 59 bottom.

Finchley Cine Video Society
Pages 29 bottom, 68 all, 69 top.

Lino Manfrotto & Co.,
Pages 16 both.

Panasonic (UK) Ltd.,
Pages 9 top and bottom left.

Chris Priest
Page 11 bottom.

Sanyo (UK) Ltd.,
Page 9 right.

Duncan Say.
Pages 44 top, 65 all.

Sharp Electronics (UK) Ltd.,
Pages 10 top, 2.

Small World Media
Page 28, 70 top.

Sony (UK) Ltd.,
Page 12.

Ralph Stephenson
(Woodvale Television Projects)
Pages 4, 6, 7 top, 13 top, 14 top, 18 bottom, 19 bottom both, 20 both, 21 top, 23 all, 24 bottom, 25 all, 26, 27, 29 top, 31 top, 32-41, 49 right, 52 bottom, 58 bottom, 59 top, 60 all, 64 top left, bottom left, 67 top, 69 middle and bottom left, 70 bottom, 71 top, 73 all, 75 bottom, 174-185 (inc).

Norman Tozer
Pages 8, 17 bottom left, 18 top, 19 top, 21 bottom, 22, 31 bottom both, 42 top, 43 bottom, 45 top left, right, bottom left, 48, 49-52 top and middle, 53-57, 58 top, 61 bottom, 62 top, 63 bottom left, 66 all.

Vivanco (UK) Ltd.,
13 bottom, 14 bottom, 15, 72 top.

Simon Wallace
Page 2,

The author wishes to acknowledge the assistance of Ralph Stephenson in the preparation of the text, especially the section on News.